CRAFTY CHICA'S

ART

de la

SOUL

ALSO BY
Kathy Cano Murillo

Making Shadow Boxes and Shrines

La Casa Loca

The Crafty Diva's D.I.Y. Stylebook

The Crafty Diva's Lifestyle Makeover

Kathy Cano Murillo

CRAFTY CHICA'S

ART
de la
SOUL

Glittery Ideas
to Liven Up
Your Life

Illustrations by Patrick Murillo   Photography by John Samora

rayo   An Imprint of HarperCollinsPublishers

CRAFTY CHICA'S ART DE LA SOUL. Copyright © 2006 by Kathy Cano Murillo.
All rights reserved. Printed in China. No part of this book may be used or reproduced
in any manner whatsoever without written permission except in the case of
brief quotations embodied in critical articles and reviews. For information, address
HarperCollins Publishers, 10 East 53rd Street, New York, NY 10022.

HarperCollins books may be purchased for educational, business, or sales promotional use.
For information, please write Special Markets Department, HarperCollins Publishers,
10 East 53rd Street, New York, NY 10022.

FIRST EDITION

Book design by Shubhani Sarkar

Printed on acid-free paper

Library of Congress Cataloging-in-Publication Data
Cano Murillo, Kathy.
    Crafty Chica's art de la soul : Glittery ideas to liven up your life / by Kathy Cano Murillo ;
illustrations by Patrick Murillo ; photography by John Samora. — 1st ed.
        p.   cm.
        ISBN-10: 0-06-078942-5   ISBN-13: 978-0-06-078942-8
        1. Handicraft.   2. Decoration and ornament—Latin America—Themes, motives.
3. Decoration and ornament—Mexico—Themes, motives.   I. Title: Art de la soul.   II. Title.
TT157.C2183   2006
745.—dc22   2005044333

06   07   08   09   10   ❖/TOP   10   9   8   7   6   5   4   3   2   1

To my son, DeAngelo.

Thank you for blessing my life

and rockin' my world with your shiny, happy spirit.

And for turning me on

to the drama of professional wrestling on TV—

it makes my crafting sessons all the more exciting.

I love you!

Who is a crafty chica?

- ✤ She is clever, creative, chic, and a little quirky.
- ✤ She wears paint spills and glue-gun burns with pride and honor.
- ✤ She takes naughty pleasure in slapping fresh paint on raw wood.
- ✤ She sprinkles words like "craftylicious" and "glitteresque" in her language.
- ✤ She doesn't shell out a lot of cash to make ultra-hip stuff.
- ✤ She alters the rules with lots of imagination.
- ✤ She loves the smell of Magic Markers, especially the fruity ones.
- ✤ She turns blah into *bling!* and scraps into *cha-ching!*
- ✤ She doesn't feel guilty about occasionally using the "official" directions.
- ✤ She knows any mistake can become a masterpiece.
- ✤ She uses collage for self-therapy.
- ✤ She appreciates and originates, while others imitate.
- ✤ She spreads the gospel of art wherever she goes.
- ✤ She uses ordinary tools for extraordinary purposes.
- ✤ She maybe has yet to do any of the above, but really, really wants to.

Being a crafty chica is good thing. It's not only about flexing your creativity muscle; it's also a lifestyle—a mission statement that celebrates all things handmade and heartfelt. Even if you don't know the difference between matte varnish and spray glitter, *don't worry!* As long as you relate to any of the above descriptions, you're in the club.

Contents

Introduction

PEOPLE ALWAYS ASK HOW LONG I'VE BEEN INTO ARTS AND CRAFTS. THEY ASSUME I WAS BORN WITH A SILVER PAINTBRUSH IN MY MOUTH.

Actually, it's the opposite.

My friends gasp when I share my pitiful stories of early art rejections, like how throughout grade school, I never had a project worthy enough to adorn the coveted walls of the school's cafeteria. I was shocked—I thought I was the next junior Picasso. I reveled in the rejection and the internal torture of being a lonely, misunderstood *artista,* whose exuberant message was falling on numb eyeballs. And then came high school. I took an entry-level crafts class and scored a C on my report card.

A *C?*

Even more torment to be expressed through powdered tempera paints and Pentel markers!

Both experiences dampened my self-esteem. I knew I could work magic with my art supplies, but I didn't have concrete evidence to back it up. I didn't let that stop me from whipping up such things as a nifty (if not lumpy) faux-stained-glass wind chime, but I didn't dare show anyone for fear of, once again, being deemed mediocre. So I became a closet crafter. It was my corny little secret. I craved any downtime so I could retreat to my bedroom, crank up some reggae tunes on my Walkman, and, well, craft it up. It didn't matter if I sucked or not, I was having too much fun because there was no stuffy teacher to grade me. I set up a card table next to my bed, where I decoupaged pictures of fancy flamenco dancers on papier-mâché boxes. I topped them off with sparkly gems, feathers, and shiny varnish.

Time stopped when I was at that art table. I didn't notice if it was day or night, if anyone else was in the house, or even if the phone rang. I was in my own mesmerizing groove. When my pals came over, I invited them to take a seat in my crafty captain's chair and give the magical table a try. They became hooked as well. I had just dived into my Mexican-American heritage and used it as the foundation for my work. I was frustrated at the lack of home décor and jewelry items on the market, so I made my own line using Lotería bingo cards, images of Frida Kahlo and low rider pop art. I eventually said, "the heck with it" and began passing out my goods to whoever showed an interest. It was a rush to see the delighted look on people's faces when they opened my gifts.

It became so addicting that I began carting my treasures in my purse. I passed out painted magnets and beaded bracelets to anyone who showed interest: strangers at the library, clerks at the Department of Motor Vehicles, and bank tellers. The trunk of my tangerine BMW morphed into a makeshift showroom of tie-dye shirts and hand-crafted bags. My kitschy crafts were a hit!

But, they weren't by any means masterpieces. I had my memorable mishaps. Like the time I colored wood beads with a paint pen and gave them out, only to have my friends tell me the ink rinsed off onto their bodies while they were in the shower. I once baked clay necklace pieces that looked so yummy, a friend of mine actually ate one by accident. It didn't curb the enthusiasm. It wasn't the actual item that made them smile. It was the happy energy that I put into making it.

I've come a long way since then. My art and crafts have exploded into canvases, scrapbooks, decoupaged pottery, sculpted clay jewelry, and my latest obsession, embellished mannequin heads! I have my own kooky recipe for crafty concoctions and I write books about them, teach workshops, and sell them all over the country with my husband, who is also an artist.

The bliss extends beyond the tangible. As a woman, I've used art to express my strength. As a Latina, I've used it to connect to my culture. As a mom, wife, and daughter, I've used it to pre-serve memories of my family and to honor my ancestors. This is what being a crafty chica is all about.

And this book is my gift to you—to help you tap into your creative juicy juices and put them in overdrive. It's immersed in Latino culture because that's what I know best, and I want to share. The ideas are in true *mestizo* style, a blending of history, regions, themes, pop culture, and trendy applications. I'll show you how to make do-it-yourself décor on the cheap, with million-dollar results. You'll pick up ideas on using art for self-reflection and growth, making chic home accents and groovy gifts for your favorite *amigas*. There are tips on everything from starting a personal journal to kicking off your own local crafting group. I'll even share some of my personal experiences for you to laugh at and learn from.

Ready? Let's get this party started. And by the way—you are not being graded!

Crafty Overview

YOUR MISSION AS OF THIS MOMENT, IS TO GET CRAFTY BY ANY MEANS. MAKE ART AN IMPORTANT PART OF YOUR LIFE, JUST LIKE EATING LUNCH EVERY DAY OR downing a double latte. It won't be long before you see the world with a new set of eyes and develop a knack for details ("Wow, check out the definition of the leaves on that tree!").

Whether you are a pro or a novice, there is a whole new universe to tinker with. Your art-filled planet can be whatever you want. Consider it your personal playground with infinite possibilities. Sure, it sounds intimidating at first, but I'm here to break it down, crafty chica style. Check out the categories below and find one that suits your style. And remember, you don't have to be mysterious, serious, trendy, trained or obscure to come up with a stylish, innovative idea. As long as you are willing to put in the energy, anything can come out of those fantastic fingertips!

Collage/Decoupage

Collage and decoupage is all about assembling objects in a random but symmetrical fashion. As kids, we cut out pictures from magazines and glued them to construction paper. It was fun then, and it still is now. Collage art can be as simple or complex as you like. From designing a sleek scrapbook page to creating a cluttered *ofrenda* (altar) to your *abuela* on the fireplace mantel, it's all about balance. Basic collage is also a great "me time" hobby. Because you are only using a glue stick, paper, and scissors, it's mess-free and can be easily stored and unpacked at a moment's notice. Decoupage is about incorporating that collage onto surfaces such as plates, boxes, and tables—and then coating them with a thick, durable varnish. If you love paper collage, try the Girly-girl Photo Book on page 172.

Paper and Assemblage Arts

These are branches on the collage family tree. With paper arts, collage is combined in a functional manner to create greeting cards, books, frames, jewelry, and more. Assemblage art is collage on a dimensional level—think shadow boxes, shrines, and mixed media. These projects are a bit more complicated, but just as rewarding. You'll need to clear some space on your kitchen table, as well as your calendar (a few hours at a time). Interested? Check out the My Favorite Things Table Collage on page 25.

Tin

In Mexico, tin from old cans and containers are cycled into gorgeous rustic mirror frames, *nichos* (small window boxes), and mixed-media pieces. If you want to go the authentic route, visit a local grocery store or market to pick up imported food cans and texturize them with pliers or crimpers. If you want the tin look without the hassle, craft stores carry a wide range of ready-to-make products including rolls of brass, tin, and copper, as well as tools to embellish them. If tin tickles your fancy, you'll love the Tin Flower Mirror on page 154.

Needle Arts

Growing up, I watched my mom work her magic on the sewing machine, my Auntie Linda embroider like an Olympic contender, and my nana crochet as if thread was going out of style. These days, needle arts are at a new level of craftiness. Sure, there will always be dresses, pillows, and Halloween costumes to make, but now there is "fiber arts." Basically, it's a ritzy term for more of the same, except now artists are combining textiles with collage art, as well as embellishing ho-hum wearables. Look at the Flamenco Fringe Tanks on page 76 and you'll get the gist.

Decorative Painting

Old-school paintbrush and acrylics will never go out of style! That's because you can apply them to just about anything and end up with spectacular results. It's also one of the most cost-effective crafts to embrace. One of my guilty pleasures is to shop in the bric-a-brac section of the thrift store and choose wood bowls, canisters, boxes, and frames. It's so easy and satisfying to give them new life with rich, succulent colors. Once they are painted and varnished, they'll look like gourmet-boutique-worthy artifacts. The Wonderfuly Worn Flower Fence on page 126 is proof of that.

Everything Else

Mosaics, candles, beads, and even food art ideas await you. Once you absorb the basics mentioned above, you can be daring and whip up a batch of Aztec Body Fondue from page 94 for your boy toy, or even learn how to make your own elegant café kitchen shade with iron and fabric!

Getting in the Mood

Think you can't fit art in your schedule? Think again. When I talk to a lot of women about what holds them back, it's always lack of time. There are clothes to fold, long work hours, riveting reality TV shows to watch…Ultimately, the crafty hour is put at the bottom of the to-do list. If this is you, move it on up, chica! Don't feel guilty about devoting a few minutes a week to expressing yourself. Incorporating creativity into your life will take the edge off of stress, surge your spirit with girl-power self-esteem, and give you something cool to show off to your *comadres* and colleagues. But only you can take that first step. Here are some tips of getting in the artsy frame of mind.

1. **Keep a daily journal.** Pick up a blank book, the kind with the thick creamy pages that are thirsty for your thoughts. Decorate the cover with gems, sequins, ribbons, and letters. Give your journal a catchy name; make it your new best friend. Force yourself to write something or doodle every day. Don't think about it. Unplug that flashing sign called "common sense" and just let your imagination flow on the pages like soft-serve ice cream. Jot down quotes that made you raise your eyebrows, attach pictures and write up funny captions for them, pick up a leaf from the park and insert it in the back pages, use colored markers to practice a new way of signing your name. Fill each page with your wish list of the day, and pick one to focus on. Carry

it with you and ask your friends to sign it like a yearbook. Keep a special page to write down your ideas for projects.

2. **Plan ahead to get crafty.** This doesn't mean to punch in "8 a.m. Saturday: Be creative" in your Blackberry. All it means is to pick a project and chew on it for a couple days. See if you have the supplies in your house: if not, add the craft store to your list of errands. Look at the week ahead and pinpoint a block of time when you can get rolling. Even if it means waking up two hours early one morning, do it.

3. **Think portable.** If you only have little pockets of time available, choose beading, crochet, or journaling, projects that can be tucked inside a small purse. These crafts are perfect for when you are waiting for your next class to start, or you're stuck in a doctor's office waiting room or at a boring party. OK, maybe not that last one!

4. **Join a local crafty group.** I call it "Craft n Chat." Check out the local paper or Internet message boards to find "meet ups" for crafting or Stitch N Bitches, for knitting or crochet. This is where people of similar interests get together on a regular basis and gossip, gab, or gloat about

their lives and others. These groups always welcome newbies. Better yet, check out page 177 to learn how to start your own craft group.

5. **Take a class.** Some people need a structured environment and that's just fine. From chain stores to mom-and-pop shops, there are workshops galore on every technique and theme under *el sol*. Stained glass, mosaics, jewelry making—you name it, there's a class for it. If you want a flexible alternative, visit a local scrapbook store where they have open labs. You simply pay a small fee to use their supplies, and there is always an instructor around to help. Classes are a great way to "sample" different genres. Once you find one that connects with your personality, you'll know exactly what supplies to invest in.

6. **Have a crafty chica party.** *Woo-hoo!* Call a couple friends and invite them over to make an easy craft, such as greeting cards. Buy a box of blank cards, scissors, and glue and tell everyone to bring embellishments to share. At the end, swap them with each other.

7. **Set up a cozy corner.** Cozy corners are vital to peace of mind. Don't let anyone tell you different. You don't even have to craft there; it's just a comfy area in your home that feels calm and soothing. Find a nook in a room, a cushy chair, a soft throw, and a rug that feels sumptuous between your toes. This is a place for you to sip your favorite tea, read magazines, paint your nails, listen to your iPod, indulge in a good book, or just shut your eyes and pretend you are in a Cuban café listening to a percussionist. While you're there, you might as well pick up a set of knitting needles and yarn!

8. **Take a spontaneous field trip.** Have the frump-girl blues? Fight it. Pick a place that is off your radar and go there. I guarantee you'll become inspired again. Try window-shopping at the most expensive mall in the city, visit a coffeehouse in an uncharted neighborhood, go to an author signing for a book you never heard of, check out the closest cluster of antique shops, visit a local gallery, or sit on a park bench and people-watch. Heck, just go to a bookstore and grab a stack of design magazines and books. Flip through them and buy the ones that made you think "Hmmm, I can do that!" Spontaneous field trips infuse your mind with new faces, colors, and ideas.

9. **Surf the Web.** Open your favorite search engine and type in "hip crafts" or whatever topic you

are curious about, such as "altered art" or "fabric collage." You can also sign up for crafty forums where you can mingle with other crafty ladies and share ideas.

10. **Visit a new area at the craft store.** It's easy to get pigeonholed into one type of hobby. If you are into making scrapbooks, then you probably know that area of the store like the back of your paper cutter. For one day, ditch the obvious. Visit the kid's area, the yarn section, the framing department. Chances are you'll learn something new!

Diary of a Crafty Chica

My name is Kathy and I'm a craftaholic. In one month, I make an average of fifty or sixty art projects. I've never encountered a clearance shelf I didn't like. I was once robbed at the craft store because I was too involved inspecting the metallic threads to notice that someone lifted my wallet from my purse. Basically, I'm not perfect.

While 95 percent of my endeavors come out with stunning results, I'm not afraid to admit the glitches. All of us have them and we shouldn't be ashamed. I call them my *chica loca* moments—when you reflect on an experience and say, "What was I thinking?" *Chica loca* moments aren't just about art. They can sprout from anywhere: craft projects gone bad, relationships, shopping, cooking, anything. You'll notice each chapter begins with a diary entry, where I share these humbling exploits. Kind of like a Latina Bridget Jones with a glue gun.

When you are done making fun of me, it's time to reflect on your *chica loca* memories. At the back of the book are blank pages to write your own adventures. Because as crafty chicas, we must learn to embrace the good—and somehow find a positive lesson in the not so good.

In order to make art from the soul, you have to be in touch with your soul. So go sit in your cozy corner and take time to answer these questions—from your *corazón*. When you're finished, use them as the foundation for making the projects in this book or for entries in your journal.

1. I wish I could do more of these activities because they make me happy: _____ _____ _____

2. If there were a sitcom about my alter-ego life, it would be about a chica who lives with _____ _____, works at _____ _____, and wants to become a _____.

3. The wackiest thing I've ever done in all my life is: _____

4. These people inspire me: _____ _____

5. The three things I'm most proud of in my life are: _____

6. By this time next year, this is what I want to be doing with my life: _____ _____ _____

7. If I could get a $1,000 gift certificate to be used only on me, I would go shopping for: _____ _____ _____ _____

8. Most people don't know this surprising fact about me: _____ _____ _____

9. I should be featured on *Oprah* for my success with my: _____ _____ _____

10. My dream vacation involves _____, _____, and lots of _____.

11. If I could replace a leading lady in any film, it would be _____ in _____ because _____.

12. The one thing I wish I had more of in my life is _____. In order to do that, I have to _____.

13. This is my mission statement of my life: _____ _____ _____

14. A hundred years from now, I want to be remembered for: _____ _____ _____

15. I've procrastinated on this too long! As of tomorrow I'm going to get started on: _____ _____ _____

Setting Up Shop

To make the most of your talents, you have to be slightly organized. Here are some trusty guidelines when it comes to Crafting 101.

Create a workspace. Locate a cheery area in your house and deem it your home base for all things handmade. It doesn't have to be permanent. It can be as easy as a card table and a tote box of supplies. Invest in a desktop task lamp to aid your peepers, and an extension cord and outlet strip for multiple tools (dual glue guns, embossing gun, Dremel, etc.), and keep a TV or radio close by to keep you entertained. Put on something like Ozomatli or Andrea Echeverri so you can shimmy your shoulders while you create.

Sort your supplies. Use clear plastic boxes with bold labels (markers, rubber stamps, etc.). If you are really serious and are setting up a permanent craft space, use shelving units and file cabinets to hold containers. Decorate the blank labels with colored markers and add swirlies and zigzag designs to make the box look festive.

Have a main crafty toolbox. This is to hold all the necessities: scissors, measuring tape, paintbrush, glue, paper towel, craft knife, cup to hold water, yarn, tape, pins, etc. Decorate the box with bright paint, metallic pens, glitter glue, and stickers to make it look like a chest of *tesoros*.

Shop wise. Look through the local newspaper or Web sites for coupons and sales. Check your local yellow pages for supply warehouses that are open to the public. Scour the listings on eBay for bulk supplies. Check in with your friends and see if there are any supplies you can swap.

Keep a notebook. Write down what you made, the items you used, and where you bought them. Keep track of any mistakes or pleasant surprises. Jot down new ideas and sketches. Keep your notebook with your supplies so it will be there when you need it. If you can, take pictures of your completed items and tape them into the notebook.

Supplies, Supplies, Supplies

Supplies are the tangible tools to your success! Hold them, inspect them, love them, and appreciate them. Do this, and they will reward you handsomely. Here is a rundown of all the materials used in the following pages. You *don't* need all of them, but it's good to know what's out there for use in future projects.

Delta Ceramcoat water-based acrylics: These are excellent non-toxic paints. They provide great coverage on any kind of surface and come in more than a hundred shades. Tip: Always rinse the paint off your brush when you aren't using it. If you spill it on clothing, immediately wash it out with water; otherwise it will stain. To avoid this, take a big, roomy T-shirt and make it your official "paint shirt." That way if you do spill, you won't have to worry.

Dimensional squeeze paint: This paint is in a squeeze bottle that squirts out like icing. I love to use the crystal colors on top of the flat paint to add more definition to the overall look.

Varnish: Naturally, you want your work to last forever, so varnish is *muy importante.* I go back and forth between two kinds—spray-on, and water-based polyurethane. Spray-on is good for outdoor projects. Choose from high-gloss or matte and then, working outside, spray on the item, let it dry, and add a second coat. Water-based polyurethane is applied with a brush and is best for lightweight or paper projects. It can be used inside and cleans up easily with water and a paper towel.

Pens: These are great to have around when you want to add sharp lines but are too chicken to use the paintbrush. They also are a must-have for paper projects. The ones I use are metallic paint pens and fine-line Sharpie permanent markers.

Glitter: To make your project *pop!* apply loose micro glitter over wet paint, tap off the excess on a piece of paper, and pour it back in the jar. There are several options for using glitter in your art:

- ✴ **Squeeze glitter:** Dimensional squeeze paint that sparkles when it's dry.
- ✴ **Polyester microfine glitter:** This is my favorite; it's like crushed crystals and looks ever so elegant.
- ✴ **Delta sparkle varnish:** This is a glossy sealer that can be painted on any surface. It goes on milky, but dries to a clear finish with tiny translucent flecks.
- ✴ **Glitter spray:** If you really want to go overboard, try this stuff that comes in a can. But use caution: it comes out very wet and will warp paper projects if you don't follow the package directions.
- ✴ **Loose glitter:** This is the old favorite we used in art class. It's still around and it still does the job.

Adhesives: This is where many crafters get confused. What glue works best? Actually, there are different glues for a variety of purposes...kind of like cooking oils. One size does not fit all.

✣ **E6000:** Comes in a silver tube and bonds anything known to man—metal, wood, plastic. Dries to a clear rubbery finish. It does have a slight odor. If you are sensitive, go for Crafter's Pick the Ultimate.

✣ **Hot glue gun/high-temp sticks:** Used for attaching small objects, trims, and quick fixes. Does not bond to metal or plastic.

✣ **Elmer's white craft glue:** All-around five-star adhesive. Use it straight from the bottle for general projects, thin it down with water for papier-mâché, or use it as an under- and overcoat for decoupage projects. Dries clear.

✣ **Aleene's OK to Wash It:** For use on any fabric project. Not recommended in place of major sewing projects, but it works perfect for embellishments. And you can wash it!

✣ **Glue sticks:** Simple glue sticks for lightweight paper projects.

✣ **Terrifically Tacky double-sided tape:** This super-strength adhesive tape comes in varying widths and bonds like glue. Useful for any kind of embellishment project.

Scissors: Mini scissors, regular scissors, and decorative-edge ones will get you through. Tin snips are required for cutting through metal sheets.

Brushes: Wide foam or soft bristle brushes for base-coating large surfaces, thin liner brushes for outlining and detail.

Needlenose pliers or tweezers: These will save you when you need to crimp, hold, or pick up tiny objects.

Jump rings: These are small silver circles that come in different sizes. They are used to connect two objects and to create a "dangling" look.

Pictures, papers, rubber stamps, and stencils: There are several methods to try out.

✣ **Photos:** Personal photos make your art one-of-a-kind, but always make color copies at a copy center or on your home computer using high-quality photo paper. That way, not only will you preserve the original, but you'll also have the option of reducing and enlarging the image. Save images from calendars, books, and note cards.

✴ **Papers:** Craft stores usually have big bags of scraps, or tablets of scrapbook sheets. These are your best bet because they come in a spectrum of designs, textures, and colors. I like to go beyond that and use foreign-language newspapers, food labels, wrapping paper, gift tissue, handmade paper, corrugated board, and more.

✴ **Rubber stamps:** These are costly, but if you visit a paper arts store and sign up for open lab, you can use theirs. If you do buy your own, look on eBay for great deals. Tip: Take care of your stamps by cleaning the ink off with a non-alcohol baby wipe and then wash in warm water. Always store your stamps, rubber side down.

✴ **Inks for stamping:** It's a big deal to know your inks before you head into stamping waters. Just worry about two of them. Permanent ink dries quick, and can be used on almost all surfaces (fabric, paper, wood, glass, etc.). Pigment inks are tricky. They work best on matte paper, or glossy paper, as long as you emboss it. Otherwise, the ink will never dry. If you aren't embossing, always go with permanent ink.

✴ **Embossing powder:** This is a highly concentrated powder that you pour over pigment-ink-stamped images, and then dry by running a heat gun over it. The powder turns to a raised shiny surface.

Fabrics: Not just for clothing anymore! Use small pieces in card making, gift wrap, collages, and other projects. Fabric stores and remnant shops have clearance and/or scrap bins where you can buy grab bags stuffed with goodies.

Found objects: These are the little odds and ends that normal people toss out. Not us! Buttons, keys, labels, charms, old earrings, etc.: they all have a place and purpose.

Sequins, beads, gems, and rhinestones: Sparkles are the spice of life when it comes to arts and crafts. It doesn't mean you have to go all "Cher" on your project, but a little hint of the twinkly never hurts.

Threads and yarns: Fibers are fabulous and functional. Use thick chunky ones to outline larger projects and fine one for small tasks. They can be glued, sewn, gathered, and woven to add a dash of color to your work.

One morning when I was having breakfast with my crafty friends, our conversation wandered from the high price of gasoline to the subject of soldered picture jewelry. We eventually polished off our pancakes and cappuccinos, paid, and departed on our separate ways.

I walked to my car with the vigor of a woman on a mission. I was to spend the day making dozens of these so-called soldered picture necklaces, and they would be fabulous. But I needed microscope slides and thin copper tape: Two items the craft stores had yet to carry. So, on the way home, I stopped at a hobby shop.

The bell rang above my head as I entered. I glanced at the multitude of shelves that were stacked with model car, airplane, and science project kits. "Hmm, it's a craft store for boys!" I thought. "How cute!"

Behind the stainless steel counter was an elderly man with bifocals. Stocking the shelves behind him was a teen that could have passed for Napoleon Dynamite's twin. I politely requested my microscope slides and copper tape. The man slid the package of slides across the counter and mumbled that they didn't carry copper tape.

"Darn! I thought for sure you would have it here," I replied.

"Whatcha using it for?" he deadpanned as he peered over his thick lenses. I began to tell him about my grand plan for soldered picture necklaces, but he stopped me midsentence.

"You need to go to an arts and crafts store," he said, shaking his hand in the air, as to dismiss me. "We don't carry

> 'You need to go to an arts and crafts store,' he said, shaking his hand in the air, as to dismiss me. 'We don't carry any stuff like that here. We only carry stuff for rockets, airplanes, cars . . . No jewelry stuff. No crafts.'

any stuff like that here. We only carry stuff for rockets, airplanes, cars...No jewelry stuff. No crafts."

I tried to explain that copper tape was not part of the normal jewelry-making process, that it was actually used in plumbing (I think), and that it's not sold at craft stores. Again he interrupted: "No crafts!" he snapped.

I looked down to grasp my purse. Next to it was a point-of-purchase display rack of plastic stained-glass kits with cheesy patterns of kitties and frogs.

"Um. Aren't these crafts?" I asked, pointing to them.

Right then, the Napoleon nerd lifted the counter's flap and stepped out to meet me face-to-face. "We're phasing those out. Anything else we can help you with, ma'am?" The two of them waited for my reply, hoping I would get lost and take my girly-girl cooties with me.

Suddenly, soldered picture necklaces weren't important. Standing up for my crafty dignity was.

"As a matter of fact, there is something else I need!" I demanded.

"Huh?" the man said. "What else?"

"I'm looking for...um...a—a model car kit. Yes. I need a model car kit."

In reality, I needed a model car kit like I needed a glue-gun burn on my *nalga*. But I wasn't about to let these wanna-be *machismo* meanies get the best of me. On behalf of women crafters everywhere, I needed to prove I could do boy crafts too.

The kid smirked. Now I was their Saturday morning

> **"** I tried to explain that copper tape was not part of the normal jewelry-making process, that it was actually used in plumbing (I think), and that it's not sold at craft stores. Again he interrupted: 'No crafts!' **"**

amusement. "Oh yeah? What kind of kit? Easy, moderate, or challenging?"

Eeek, a trick question! Hobby boy code talk. Gramps leaned toward me, removed his glasses and continued the interrogation.

"Foreign or domestic? Vintage or contemporary?"

I took a deep breath and pretended I was a *Jeopardy* finalist.

"I'll take challenging, domestic, and vintage," I replied with confidence. They glanced at each other, annoyed. The kid led me to my designated section.

"This should be easy enough, I'll just grab one, pay, and get out of here," I thought. My gaze followed the clerk's pointed bony finger and gasped at what was before me: a towering wall, jam-packed with challenging, domestic, vintage car kits.

My eye caught a box featuring a 1940s Ford. It looked just like the one my husband, Patrick, used to pick me up with when we first began dating. He called it his "bomb" and it was pretty slick. My mom hated that car, but that's another story. I figured I'd get the kit for Patrick as a surprise.

"I'll take this one. I haven't made one like this before, I'm anxious to try it," I said to the men. I pulled the box from the shelf and took it to the counter. Mr. Viejo rang it up.

"So, you make these, do ya?" he asked.

"Yeah, I've tinkered with them. Everything I need is in the box, right? It's been so long since I made one."

"If you made them, you know the answer then, right?" he said.

I gave him my cash and left. I felt empowered to have had the last laugh. How dare they pull that "No crafts!" stuff with me. I hoped I had taught them a lesson about never underestimating a female crafter. I arrived home, and rushed to show Patrick my impromptu gift.

"Wow, cool! I thought you were just going to breakfast with the girls. How'd you end up with a model car? I love it," he said.

"I stopped by that little hobby store on the way home. The clerks there inspired me to buy it."

"I love that store, they have everything you need to make rockets and stuff," he commented while reading the side of the box. "Hey, did you get glue for this?"

"Glue? The sales guy didn't tell me about glue," I said.

"How dumb. Why would he sell you a kit with no glue? Everyone knows you need glue when you get these kits."

Well. So much for my last laugh. I did, however, make my microscope slide necklaces and, yes, they came out fabulous. Patrick has yet to make the model car. I've never returned to that store, although I have fantasies about doing a crafty drive-by with machine guns that spray out hot pink glitter, and confetti made from copper foil tape.

> **"** I felt empowered to have had the last laugh. How dare they pull that "No crafts!" stuff with me. I hoped I had taught them a lesson about never underestimating a female crafter. **"**

Crafty Chica's Lesson Learned: Never let anyone make you feel unworthy or silly about something you love to do. On a more technical note, call around to stores when looking for a specific product, instead of driving there first. It will save you time and money.

CHAPTER

1

TIEMPO
de
SOLEDAD

Before making art for others, create some for you.

You deserve to step out of the usual grind for a

bit, and treat yourself to the following personal

projects. Stitch, glue, and draw away the hours

to discover talents you never knew existed, and

in the end, the results will serve as a constant

reminder of accomplishment. Not to mention,

they will look *muy magnífico!*

Super Santitos Fabric Prayer Book

THERE ARE SOME THINGS MONEY CAN'T BUY. FOR EVERYTHING ELSE, THERE IS THIS LUSCIOUS FABRIC PRAYER BOOK. WHIP IT TOGETHER AND YOU ARE ONE STEP CLOSER TO HAVING ALL YOUR dreams, wishes, and prayers answered. By combining funky fabrics with Mexican prayer cards and *medallas* (medals) you'll have one heavenly page-turner.

Supplies

8 pieces of contrasting fabric, 10 by 10 inches each

1 package inkjet-printable fabric sheets

4 pieces of batting, 9½ by 9½ inches each

Assorted fabric scraps

Assorted religious images

Assorted trims

Assorted threads and/or embroidery floss

Medals, *milagros,* buttons

Sewing machine or permanent fabric glue

Scissors and straight pins

Make it

1. Print the religious images on the fabric sheets, according to package directions, and then cut them out.

2. Lay out the fabric squares; these are going to be your pages for the book. Take the images and fabric trims and arrange each page, creating a layout that you like. Pin the images and trim in place.

3. Using the fabric glue or a sewing machine, attach the images in place on all of the pages. If you want to embellish your book with embroidery or sewn-on buttons, medals, or *milagros,* do it at this stage.

4. Pair up the pages in sets of two. Insert a piece of batting between each of the sets and pin around the borders. Make sure your pages are right side up on both sides. Sew or glue the edges of the pages together. Trim the edges to your liking.

5. Line up the pages and pin along the left-hand side. Use embroidery thread to stitch the book together. To add more embellishments, use hot glue.

Tips: Use contrasting threads and stitches to give your book more dimension. Don't worry about lining everything up: this is a free-form collage, let your spontaneous creativity flow from your heart and out through your fingertips. It's OK for the pages and pictures to be crooked, or for loose threads to hang: it will give your book more character.

✳✳✳✳✳**Take It to the Next Level!** ✳✳✳✳✳

✢ Sew on an extra piece of fabric to create a pocket to hold your prayer cards, rosary, or pictures.

✢ Incorporate personal pictures or prayers by printing them out on the fabric sheets and attaching them in your book.

✢ Personalize the book to give as a gift for baptisms, weddings, or *quinceñeras*.

It's All in the Cards

Prayer and saint cards are beautiful pieces of art that will add a touch of spirituality to your work. But before you use them, do some homework—not only out of respect, but also for your own personal benefit. Here is a list of my favorites. To learn about others, visit www.catholic.org/saints.

* St. Anthony of Padua: Doctor of the Church
* St. Catherine of Bologna: Patron of artists
* St. Clare: Patron of sore eyes
* St. Francis of Assisi: Patron of animals and merchants
* St. Gerard Majella: Patron of expectant mothers
* St. Isidore of Seville: Proposed patron of Internet users
* St. James the Greater Apostle: Patron of laborers
* St. Jude: Patron of desperate causes
* St. Maria: Patron of youth
* St. Monica: Patron of wives and abuse victims
* St. Rita: Patron of impossible causes
* St. Teresa: Patron of headache sufferers
* St. Valentine: Patron of love and happy marriages
* Our Lady of Guadalupe: Patron of the Americas

My Favorite Things Table Collage

OPEN THE DRAWER TO YOUR NIGHTSTAND. SEE ALL THOSE TRINKETS AND THINGS YOU LOVE SO DEAR-LY? TAKE THEM OUT OF HIDING AND GIVE THEM THE PROPER RESPECT THEY DESERVE: PUT THEM in a silverware sorter instead! This project wins four silver stars for innovation. Think about it: a silverware sorter tucked inside a tea tray that is made into a table collage? Now that's a crafty idea.

Supplies

1 shallow wood silverware tray, approximately 17 by 12 inches

1 standard folding wood TV tray

1 tea tray with a flat top edges, approximately 19 by 14 inches

1 piece of tempered glass, ¼ inch thick, edges seamed, 19 by 14 inches

Assorted mementos that will fit inside the compartments: small dolls, toys, magnets, souvenirs, printed phrases and pictures glued to cardstock, alphabet blocks, etc.

Assorted patterned papers

Glues: E6000 industrial-strength adhesive, hot glue

Black spray paint

Spray-on varnish

Handheld drill, electric screwdriver, 1½-inch flathead screws

Double bond tape, 6 feet (purchase with the glass)

Fringe, 2 yards

Scissors, craft knife

* ⁂ *Make it* *

The Table:

1. Spray-paint the silverware tray, the tea tray, and the TV tray. Let dry. Spray on two layers of varnish, letting dry after each coat.
2. Stand the TV tray upright. Place the tea tray on top. On each inside corner of the tea tray, use the drill, screwdriver, and screws to attach the two pieces together.

The Collage:

3. Now you are going to build the collage inside the silverware tray. Using the craft knife and glue stick, line the back of each compartment of the silverware tray with contrasting papers. For a subdued look, they can be all in the same color family, but different hues. Let dry.
4. Arrange your items in the compartments to your liking. Try to create a balance of large items in one compartment and a grouping of smaller pieces in another. Once you've designed the layout you like, use the E6000 to glue the pieces in place. Let dry for 24 hours.

Assemble:

5. Lift the silverware tray and apply a generous amount to the bottom. Center it inside the table and press down to secure. Let dry for 24 hours.
6. Clean the glass so it is free of fingerprints and/or streaks. Cut and apply the bonding tape to the top edges of the tea tray. Carefully place the glass on top and press firmly around the edges. Make sure to line it up correctly because the tape will evaporate as soon as it comes in contact with the glass. Use hot glue to add fringe around the bottom of the tea tray, so it extends below the edge of the TV tray.

Tips: To keep items in place while the E6000 cures, add a drop of hot glue as well. Instead of paint, stain your table for a toned-down look. Don't try to cram everything in the compartments; if you have too many items, just create an extra table to match!

✳✳✳✳ **Take It to the Next Level!** ✳✳✳✳

✢ If you don't need an end table, create the piece inside the silverware tray, cover it with glass, and hang it as a shadow box instead.

✢ Choose a theme for your table, such as vacation trips, family heirlooms, a hobby, or a story (use each compartment for a different reference).

✢ Make it reusable. Don't glue any of the items down and don't glue down the glass. That way you can change it season by season.

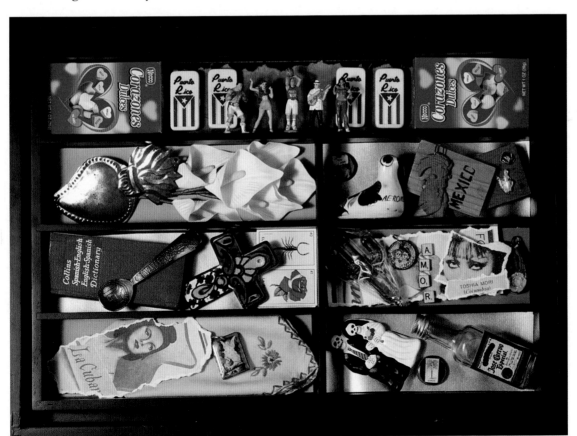

Las Mujeres Empowerment Box

WITH ALL THOSE CHORES, RESPONSIBILITIES, AND QUESTIONS TO BE ANSWERED THROUGHOUT THE DAY, WHO HAS TIME FOR INTERNAL POSITIVE REINFORCEMENT? IT'S AS THOUGH THERE needs to be a constant tap on your shoulder just to keep you focused on the good things in *tu vida*. Let this box be that reminder. After you make it, set it in a place that you see everyday—next to your alarm clock or by your makeup case. Fill it with upbeat quotes, stickers, fortune cookie notes, funny comics, and anything else that makes you smile. Every morning, pull one out and make it your mantra for the day. When things get hectic, draw on that image or saying to get you through. See someone else being a Debbie Downer? Share your daily manifesto with her or him.

Supplies

1 pine or balsa wood box with
    detachable lid
1 roll of silver embossing tin
1 disposable ballpoint pen
E6000 industrial-strength
    adhesive
1 knob

4 wood balls
Acrylic paint, paintbrush
Favorite quotes printed or
    written on small pieces of
    decorative paper
Scissors

Make it

1. Paint the inside and bottom of the box, as well as the wood balls. Let dry.
2. Working on a flat work area, unroll the embossing tin and smooth it out flat with your hands.
3. Cover one side of the box with a thin layer of E6000, and set it on the far left side of the sheet of tin, leaving a quarter inch border at the side and bottom. Press the box in place. You will be covering the remaining sides by using a continuous piece of tin. Hold the box down and cover the next side with E6000. Carefully roll the box over again. Press in place. Repeat until all the sides are covered. Trim off the excess. Let dry. Fold the quarter inch border over to cover the inner lip of the box and glue in place to create a polished look.
4. Cover the lid by smoothing the remaining tin out on a table, applying glue to the top and sides of the lid,

and laying it top down on the tin. Press firmly in place. Cut around the edges, leaving enough tin to cover the sides and inner lip. Fold up the tin on each side. Rub the surface hard with your fingers to make sure it bonds to the wood. Let dry. Drill a hole in the center and attach the knob.

5. Pressing very hard, use the ballpoint pen to draw designs on the tin. To transfer a picture, set the image on the tin, and lightly go over the lines with the pen. Lift the paper and retrace the design using bold lines. Repeat to decorate the rest of the box. Flip the box upside down and glue on the wood balls. Let dry.

6. Fold the quotes up individually and put them in the box.

Tips: Use cheap scissors and pens because this project will ruin them. To hold the tin in place while the glue dries, use rubber bands.

✳✳✳✳**Take It to the Next Level!**✳✳✳✳

✳ Rub textured objects over the tin to add bumps and grooves or use stencils to draw the designs.

✳ Use glass paint to add vibrant color to your box.

✳ Choose a favorite poem and write it on the outside of the box.

✳ Use this method to decorate any soft wood items, such as magnets, picture frames, even the head-board of your bed!

Step Out of the Box

Tired of being as predictable as darts on a wedding dress? Maybe it's time to shake up your life, take a risk, do something daring. It doesn't mean you have to go bungee jumping with your *primos locos,* but you can at least change your soft drink once in a while. Loosen up and let go! Here are some easy ways to make your friends say, "You did *what* today?"

* Put some chunky highlights in your hair.
* If your hair is straight, wear it curly. Or vice versa.
* Wear false eyelashes and Cleopatra eyeliner for a day.
* Apply glitter dust to your chest and cheeks.
* Next time you dine out, order the last thing you would ever think of eating.
* Put in an application for your favorite reality TV show.
* Rent a Hummer for half a day.
* Write a poem and recite it at open mic night.
* Leave a secret note for a friend. Sign it *"Señora Mysteriosa."*
* Go up to the mean person in the office or classroom and give them a compliment.
* Open the dictionary, pick an unusual word, and use it throughout the day.
* Make up a dance to go with your favorite song. Teach it to your friends next time you party together.
* Buy a cool box of postcards (better yet, make them!), sign them with a happy message, and mail them to your favorite people.
* Take a different route when you travel to work or school.

Nana to the Rescue

My respect for sewing came from my Nana Cano, the super-woman of all things domestic. I was to be a bridesmaid at my brother's wedding. Like so many *chicas* before me, I ignored the warnings about preordering my custom-made dress two sizes smaller. I was an overachiever. I figured I'd easily shave off a cool twenty-five pounds in time for that classy glide down the aisle in front of the three-hundred plus attendees.

Two weeks before the final fitting, I went on my usual crash diet and dropped a size, as predicted. I was so thin I could feel my hipbones.

"Once again, mission accomplished!" I thought.

The time came for that last appointment. I went to the bridal boutique, stepped into the dressing room, and confidently slid that silky sucker over my head. But no matter how much I squirmed, I couldn't get the zipper up. I calmly called for assistance.

One of the attendants busted in the room. She took one look, wrinkled her eyelids, and frowned. She gripped my arm and whipped me around to face the wall, as if she were on bridesmaid patrol and I had committed a serious dress-altering crime.

"Suck it in," she ordered.

She then proceeded to manhandle me while conducting a wrestling match with the zipper. I held my breath in utter disbelief.

"You need to suck it in *more*. You're too fat. Did you gain weight since your last fitting?" she asked.

"No!" I shot back as I released a mouthful of air.

> **❝The time came for that last appointment. I went to the bridal boutique, stepped into the dressing room, and confidently slid that silky sucker over my head. But no matter how much I squirmed, I couldn't get the zipper up. I calmly called for assistance.❞**

> **"** I went in my room and took the dress off the hanger. I signaled for my then-obnoxious thirteen-year-old little sister to do the honors of negotiating with the evil zipper. I grabbed the door handle of the closet with one hand and made the sign of the cross with the other. **"**

"I ordered it two sizes smaller! I lost weight to fit in it, I swear. Feel my hipbones!"

"Well, it sure don't fit now," she snapped as she anchored her fists on her lumpy hips. "And we don't do refunds if you ordered it smaller. Says it in the contract. What do you want to do?"

I had one week before the wedding—just enough time for my Aztec warrior angels to perform a miracle. My only worry was to keep my slip-up from my overly inquisitive *familia.*

On the drive home, I gave myself the "everything always works out OK, so don't worry" pep talk. I walked in the house and my mom, sister, and cousin buzzed around me like flies on flan. They wanted me to model the dress. They had seen everyone in their gowns except me. I convinced them I was too exhausted, and sneaked off to bed to begin the first of seven nights of marathon prayer sessions.

The night before the wedding arrived. I had starved myself all week and managed to lose another ten pounds. My mom demanded I try on the dress. She knew something was up when I passed on the traditional rehearsal dinner earlier that evening. When Kathy skips dessert, you know something is up.

I went in my room and took the dress off the hanger. I signaled for my then-obnoxious thirteen-year-old little sister to do the honors of negotiating with the evil zipper. I grabbed the door handle of the closet with one hand and made the sign of the cross with the other. Not only for my sake, but for the reputation of my family: *"Please,"* I begged the angels of

dressmakers in the sky, *"let it fit!!!"* If it wouldn't cooperate, what could I do? Not be in the wedding? Find a stand-in? Wear a shawl? I glanced at my little sis only to see her flash me a wicked "You are in *so* much trouble" grin.

"Mommy!" she squealed as she forced up the zipper. "Kathy is too fat for her dress!"

Girl got it up all right, but in the process, everything else got squeezed up too. I didn't look like the young, svelte Natalie Wood I had originally envisioned. With two mountains of fleshy cleavage spilling out of my neckline, I looked more like Lusty Lolita from the Dunes Cocktail Lounge.

Fine for a seedy dive bar, not fine for conservative church nuptials.

I entered Mom and Dad's bedroom with my head hung and shoulders slumped. My mother gasped in horror. My father remained calm.

"Go to Nana's in the morning, she'll fix it for you," he said.

I followed his advice. The next morning, Nana whipped out her measuring tape, felt me up and down, and examined the dress down to its last fiber. She pushed her glasses up on her nose and rolled up the sleeves on her housecoat. The prognosis?

"Everything will be OK," she said. "I'll just take it apart and put it back together a bit bigger. Come back later."

To help, I purchased a $100 body wrap at a spa. I lost six inches! OK, it was from my left wrist, right knee, and both ankles—but hey, any little bit counts. I returned to Nana's and she helped me put on the dress. Thank goodness, it was a

perfect fit. Nana was my angel! Except that in her nervousness, she had accidentally sewed the backside of the dress on inside out. I wanted to cry, but I held it together.

We had three hours before I was to cross the threshold of the church. It was time for Nana and her trusty Singer to work some magic. She hopped back on the machine with *Terminator*-like determination. Under the watchful eyes of her ceramic elephant collection, I waited in the living room, trembling in my flesh-covered body girdle and chewing my acrylic nails. I witnessed the streams of sweat dripping down her petite and wrinkled forehead as she prayed and sewed. She fed the fabric to the hum of the machine, all while chanting repeatedly: "Oh please sweet Jesus, *pleeeease* let my little *mi'jita* look *beee-u-tee-ful* for the wedding!"

Thankfully, her prayers (and mine) were answered. I walked down that wedding runway with more finesse than post-pregnancy Catherine Zeta-Jones at a movie premiere. Nana Cano saved my butt. Literally.

She passed away a few years later, and naturally she was all I could think about when I received my own sewing machine. After years of serious crafting, I felt confident enough to confront the world of bobbins, foot pedals, and sewing emergencies. I had her genes in me, after all.

Crafty Chica's Lesson Learned: If the most experienced of nanas can crack under pressure, you can too. Before you approach any crafty crisis, always double-check your calculations. Whispering a little prayer under your breath won't hurt either. And never order a custom dress too small—it's much easier to take it in than to make it larger.

> **"** It was time for Nana and her trusty Singer to work some magic. She hopped back on the machine with *Terminator*-like determination. . . . I witnessed the streams of sweat dripping down her petite and wrinkled forehead as she prayed and sewed. **"**

CHAPTER

2

La

FAMILIA

Family scrapbooks can become boring with the same old birthdays, holidays, and baptisms. With all the awesome alternatives to preserving memories from gatherings, that should never happen.

Think I'm kidding? Read on, sistah!

I F YOUR FAMILY IS LIKE MINE, THERE ARE VINTAGE HANDBAGS STUFFED AT THE TOP OF THE CLOSET SHELF, FILLED WITH OLD FAMILY PHOTOS. THEY ARE SO PRICELESS, NO ONE WANTS TO MOVE THEM, or even touch them. I'm giving you permission to sneak them out for an hour to make color copies (you want to keep that aged look) so you can make a sassy bracelet like this.

Supplies

8 black-and-white copies of family photos, 1 by 1 inch each

8 pieces of patterned paper decorated with rubber stamps, 1 by 1 inch each

1 package of microscope slides

Ruler

1 small handheld glass/tile scorer and cutter (found at hardware or stained-glass store)

1 roll of copper tape (found at most paper arts or stained-glass stores)

1 roll of solder wire with rosin (found at the hardware store)

1 chunky chain bracelet, with clasp

8 jump rings, ½ inch in diameter

Photo tinting pens (optional)

1 piece of polymer clay, about the size of a large gumball

Safety goggles

Wood chopstick

Sandpaper

Solder iron

Make it

1. Put on the safety goggles. Use the ruler and the cutter to score the slide in thirds. Insert the tile in the cutter, right at the score line, and snip off the piece. Not all pieces will come out in a perfect square, but that's just fine. Continue until you have 16 one-inch glass squares. Remove safety goggles.

2. Decorate the pieces of patterned paper and color the pictures with the photo pens. Take your pictures and match each one up with a piece of the paper, because each charm will be double-sided. Sandwich the

picture and paper, right sides out, between two squares of glass. Seal the edges by applying the copper tape, making sure it looks even all the way around. Continue with remaining supplies.

3. Burnish the tape with a coin or your fingernail, to flatten any creases. The smoother the tape is, the more even the solder will look. Plug in the solder iron and let it heat up for a few minutes.

4. Lay the first charm on a flat surface. Set the roll of solder wire close by and unroll a piece. Dab the iron on the solder, hold the charm down with the chopstick, and quickly glide the solder over the copper tape. Wipe the solder iron clean on the sandpaper. Continue with all the charms, and then flip them over and do the opposite sides of each one. To do the sides, rest the charm in the ball of clay, so you will have both hands free. Let the charm cool (or use a clothespin), and then pick it up, rotate it to a new side, and continue. Repeat until all the sides are covered on all the charms.

5. Apply a thin strip of copper tape around the seam of the jump ring. Prop the charm up on the ball of clay and solder the jump ring to the top of the charm. Repeat.

6. Let the charms cool and then inspect all of them to see if any need a touch-up. It's easy to smooth out bumps: just wipe the iron clean on the sandpaper and then rest it on the spot you want to redo. As soon as the solder melts, quickly glide the iron over the area. Let cool and attach to the chunky silver link bracelet.

Tips: New to this? Expect to have a few mishaps at first. Practice makes perfect. I always cut extra squares and pictures because there is always one or two that comes out looking a little clumsy. But hey, maybe you like clumsy! In that case, just go for it! And, most important: always be careful around the iron; unplug it as soon as you are done. Keep it out of reach, so your hands or arm won't bump into it. Always use copies of original photos—no matter how great the bracelet looks, someone will be angry if you slice and dice cherished portraits! To skip the glass-cutting portion, make a necklace by sandwiching a picture between two microscope slides and soldering the edges. If you ever get really stuck, call a local stained-glass shop for advice.

❋❋❋❋**Take It to the Next Level!**❋❋❋❋

✻ Make up funny or sentimental captions for your pictures and use a glue stick to attach them to the photo.

✻ If you don't want to mess with the photo pens, just copy the pictures in color.

✻ Make a family tree bracelet by using pictures of old and young family members. Have a big family? Replace the patterned paper with more pictures.

✻ You can solder around anything—wood, ceramics, glass pebbles. Once you get the hang of it, it's easy to think of all kinds of other projects.

Loca Ropa Quilt

T-SHIRTS ARE THE HOT DOGS OF OUR CLOSETS. AND THEY MULTIPLY LIKE BUNNIES. SOME ARE EASY TO DONATE, BUT OTHERS HAVE SENTIMENTAL VALUE. WHEN THEY ARE BRAND NEW, WE ADORE them. But what happens when they wear out? I vote on their behalf—before they meet a painful, holey demise—that they be cut up and used in a family quilt. Ask each family member to submit one over-the-hill shirt from his or her collection so you can give it new life as a modern-day artifact.

Supplies

Pinking shears

18 unwanted but cool-looking T-shirts cut into 12 by 15 inch rectangles

18 fabric panels cut into 12 by 15 inch rectangles

1 flat sheet in desired color, queen-size

Batting (67 by 90 inches)

Sewing machine

Yarn and quilting needle

Straight pins

Optional: Blanket binding, appliqué embellishments

* Make it *

1. Use pinking shears to cut your T-shirts and fabric rectangles so the edges won't fray. Lay the pieces out, alternating T-shirt and fabric until you find a design you like. Pin the vertical rectangles together inside out to make six rows of six pieces.

2. Remove pins as you sew the rectangles together. Pin two completed rows together inside out and sew. Pin on the next row and sew. Continue until you have all the rows sewn together to make one large quilt top. Iron both sides.

3. Lay the sheet on the floor. Lay the batting on top of the sheet. Lay the quilt on top of the batting. Fold the edges of the sheet so it overlaps the quilt top and pin in place. Continue all the way around. Add pins throughout the center of the quilt to keep it in place. Remove the pins as you sew the border in place. Pin and then sew on the blanket binding and appliqués if desired.

4. Remove pins from the center of quilt. Thread the quilting needle with yarn and tie square knots at every other corner of the rectangles.

Tips: Replace regular fabric for the sheet. Use fabric scraps to make collages on the fabric rectangles. Some shirt designs will be smaller than others, make them uniform in size by adding trim or fabric to the edges before pinning the quilt together. Live in a cold climate? Use thicker batting. If you don't have enough shirts (or family members), don't binge on Ben and Jerry's just yet. Calm down and head to your nearest thrift store or flea market. Lazy? Geez! OK, try eBay!

❋❋❋❋Take It to the Next Level!❋❋❋❋

✢ You're a crafty chica, so think out of the rectangle! Instead of a quilt, use the T-shirt designs for other projects such as pillows or tote bags. You can even cut them up and sew them onto other shirts.

✢ Use your home computer to print family pictures, favorite quotes, or artwork on fabric sheets and then incorporate them into the quilt.

✢ Maybe make each whole row dedicated to a different person.

✢ After you make the family quilt, make one just for you. Use all of your favorite concert, travel, or sports shirts.

✢ Before pinning the quilt together, watch a chick flick and embroider on fun designs. It will take extra time, but once the quilt is finished, just think of all the props you'll get!

Family Tree in a Box

D O YOU HAVE MORE RELATIVES THAN YOU CAN COUNT? HOW IN THE WORLD CAN A CHICA KEEP THEM ALL STRAIGHT? NOT ONLY CHOOSING GIFTS, BUT EVEN JUST BRINGING UP TOPICS OF CON-versation. Enter the Family Tree in a Box. It's your decorative cheat sheet to all things relevant about *tu familia*. It works like a recipe box: each family has its own compartment, with a card for each person. The card has a picture, along with a short list of all the person's favorite things, quirks, and trivia facts. Imagine how many *pastele* points you'll score by saying things like "*Tía* Susan, I knitted a scarf for you because I know your neck gets cold this time of year. It's purple, your favorite color!"

Supplies

1 large recipe box, wood

Assorted paints, glitters, papers

Markers, rubber stamps, colored pencils

Glossy photo print paper

Photos of family members (pets included!)

Recipe divider cards

Glue stick

Make it

1. Paint and embellish the recipe box. Let dry.

2. Using a computer graphics program, crop the photos so you have a headshot of everyone. Make one card at a time. Click on the program feature to create four-by-six postcards. Place the headshot to the left, type in the family member's name, and fill out their favorite things. Print and trim to fit in the box. Repeat for remaining family members.

3. Take a family picture, preferably one with everyone in it, and adhere it to one of the recipe divider cards. Print out the name of the family and slide it into the tab.

Ideas for the Cards:

Date of birth

Favorite meal

Favorite music

Favorite movies

Likes

Hobbies

Surprising fact

Hidden talent

Tips: If you are a perfectionist, measure the inside of the box so you know exactly what size to trim your paper. To ensure even cuts, use a paper cutter. On each person's card, jot down the gifts you give them so you remember for the next year.

❋❋❋❋❋**Take It to the Next Level!**❋❋❋❋❋

❋ Rather than use the computer program, make copies of the photos and embellish each card by hand.

❋ All families have tried-and-true recipes. Take a notebook to the next family gathering and write down the recipes of the dishes. Print them on the cards and insert them in the box.

❋ Have a family craft party so everyone can make their Family Tree in a Box together.

❋ Does Dad have a hilarious kid story? Make a card for it and include it in the box.

Family Bonding Time

It's a shame that many families only unite for weddings, funerals, and holidays. Here are some tips on making the most of the time together.

* Create a family blog (an online diary) so everyone can post pictures and updates on what they are doing.
* Create an online message board on Yahoo or Google that has storage for calendars, photos, and e-mail messages.
* Have everyone send you e-mails about exciting events and compile them in a quarterly e-mail newsletter. Take turns with your siblings or cousins to compile it.
* Have everyone in the family pitch in to convert everyone's old movies into DVDs. Throw a party to watch the disc, and then pass out copies.
* Make color copies of family scrapbook pages, laminate them at the copy center, and use them as placemats for the next gathering.
* Put together a list of family trivia, make copies, and pass them out. Better yet, turn it into a quiz!
* When the kids of the family ask to put on a concert, have them invite the adults to join in.
* Put stickers under the seats of the chairs and give out prizes.
* Host a scrapbook party at your place. Make some mini-scrapbook invitations: list the time and place and supplies to bring.
* Ask your elders to share stories about their past and videotape them, use a tape recorder, or just take notes. This is to capture all the memories, straight from the person who lived them.

Cascarón Catastrophe

For the past five years, I've demonstrated a craft idea every week on the local news. It's like clockwork. I have my project, the instructions, and the demonstration goes as smooth as frosting on a cake. That is, until the Great *Cascarón* Catastrophe of 2005.

It was the Wednesday before Easter, and the usual host was on vacation. In her place was Jan, a long-time, beloved Phoenix personality. Jan is an all-around do-it-yourself queen and an Emmy award–winning journalist. She makes pasta noodles from scratch, carves ornate candles, plays classical piano, the accordion, and *mucho más.* Crowds adore her because she does it all with warmth and kindness. Did I mention she is petite, gorgeous, and playful? No wonder Arizona loves her so much!

Leave it to me to be the one that hit her on the head *six* times.

On live TV.

With eggs.

Here's how it went down:

My segment was about *cascarones,* beautiful hand-decorated confetti-filled eggs meant to be playfully crunched on people's heads. The set director made Jan and me sit outside at a picnic bench, in front of a cheery background of flowers and trees. Before the cameras rolled, Jan and I decided we would have fun and crack the eggs on each other's heads on the air. At first I was reluctant. I didn't want to be seen smashing an object on a popular, respectable TV star. But Jan's energy is so upbeat, I agreed.

> **Before the cameras rolled, Jan and I decided we would have fun and crack the eggs on each other's heads on the air. At first I was reluctant. I didn't want to be seen smashing an object on a popular, respectable TV star. But Jan's energy is so upbeat, I agreed.**

One second before the red light came on, she said, "Kathy, make it look like a surprise!"

"OK," I replied. "I'll tell you, 'Hey Jan, look over there!' and I'll point to the left."

"Great, Kath!" she said.

We went on with the segment, and after I finished the details of how to make the eggs, I pointed to the sky and threw out my "Hey Jan, look over there!" line. Her eye line moved from the camera to my finger, and I tapped her head with the hollow confetti egg. It didn't break.

So I hit her head again. Harder. I was nervous because I was on live TV and wanted my craft to work. For that instant, I forgot it was a human head that I was belting with all my might. It could have been the edge of a frying pan for all I remember. I just wanted my craft to work, that's all . . .

But the darn egg still didn't crack! I was confused because I make these eggs every year and never had a problem. I had been *Punk'd* by the universe.

At that point, Jan got a tad defensive.

"HEY!" she hollered as she grabbed an egg and hit my head. Her egg didn't crack either. She tried again. Harder. In the next instant, we both beat each other's heads with these fancy painted eggs until, finally, they cracked open and we were left with pretty, shiny sequins all over our hair—and nervous grins on our faces.

Jan was about to wrap up the segment and picked up another egg. I assumed it was a signal for Round 2. I also lifted

an egg, and hit it on her head. It didn't crack! Again—I tried two more times. She hit me on the head with her egg; that one didn't break either. She had had enough. She raised her tanned, manicured hand up to her head and yelled, "Ooooowww! That hurts!!!" And the cameras cut away.

Jan is so sweet. On the commercial break she said everything was fine and smiled at me, and the floor director whisked her off to the next segment. I stood there, alone—a plus-size crafty bully. I cleaned up my mess and the security guard walked up to the table and broke the silence.

"Wow. You gals really got into it," he said.

I didn't respond. Instead I hustled to the car and called Patrick, my husband. He answered the phone with one word: "BRUTAL!"

I cringed. "Oh no! Was it really?"

He released a whistle through his teeth and laughed. "Girl, it was BRU-*tal*! They should have had sound effects from the *Psycho* shower scene."

I hung up with Patrick and dialed my sister Theresa, who was, um, just as supportive.

"I bet she has head trauma! You hit her *Hard.* Over and *Over,* Kathy!"

I made my way back to my desk in the office. I immediately called the TV station and asked to please check that Jan was OK. The nice receptionist said, "Oh wow, Kathy! Now that was great TV! Don't worry, they were just eggshells!"

Needless to say, I was embarrassed. I'm triple Jan's size and must have looked like Lenny from *Of Mice and Men:*

" I made my way back to my desk in the office. I immediately called the TV station and asked to please check that Jan was OK. The nice receptionist said, 'Oh wow, Kathy! Now that was great TV! Don't worry, they were just eggshells!' **"**

"Aagh, purdy eggs. Me like to smash on head" (*arms outstretched like a mummy . . .*).

My co-workers had plenty to say as well: "Kathy, I can just imagine what some viewers must have thought. Things like, 'Gee! Those Mexicans are so violent! ' '" Later in the day, one of my editors asked me if I could please hit another editor over the head with my eggs. I had become the *cascarón* hit lady.

Crafty Chica's Lesson Learned: Whether you are a newbie or a pro, never take your finished projects for granted. If giving or showing off a craft you made, test it out first. With cascarones, squeeze the egg with your hand at the same time you tap it on your victim's head. It is much less humiliating. Even if it is good TV.

CHAPTER

3

La
COCINA
BUENA

In many ways, crafting is a lot like cooking. There are ingredients to gather, instructions to follow, and the outcome is something to show off and share. Here are three ways to add an artistic splash to the most popular area in the house.

Café Kitchen Window Shade

IF YOU THINK BLINDS ARE BORING AND CURTAINS ARE TOO CURVY, THINK FLAT. AS IN A ROLLER SHADE THAT YOU CAN TUG UP AND DOWN AT WILL. BY ADDING YOUR FAVORITE FABRIC TO THE usual installation hardware, you'll have a flavorful focal point to cook to.

Supplies

1 window shade kit

HeatnBond UltraHold (fusible webbing), 2–3 yards (more if needed)

Fabric, 2–3 yards (more if needed)

Sequined fringe trim

Large tassel with rope

Hot glue

Iron

Large soft table covering

Cotton pillowcase

Measuring tape

Rotary cutting tool, or scissors

Make it

1. Measure:
   * The width of the inner area of the window, allowing approximately 1½ inches on each side for the hardware for the shade.
   * The length of the window and how far you want the shade to hang. Convert this into yards, so you can purchase the fabric (remember, 36 inches, or 3 feet, in a yard).
   * The fabric to fit the above measurements, leaving an extra half inch to each side.

2. Unroll the fusible webbing on a large table or countertop so it is nice and smooth. Measure and mark off the window's dimensions. Wait—don't cut! Double-check your figures, just to make sure! OK, set? Cut at where your marks are. Set it aside.

3. Now lay the fabric, front-side down, on the table. Lay the fusible webbing (bonding side down) in the center of the fabric. Smooth out any creases with your hands. Make sure everything looks even.

4. Heat up the iron to a cotton setting. Lay the pillowcase over the fusible webbing and set the iron in the center. Do not move it in a back-and-forth motion. Instead, press firmly, lift, and press, working outward

to the edges. When you have covered the entire area, repeat. Let cool. Flip the fabric over, right side up. It will now be fused to the fusible webbing and will be thick and stiff.

5. Now iron again, this time on the front side of the fabric to ensure it is completely affixed to the webbing. Lay the pillowcase on the fabric and repeat the ironing process. Let cool and then rub your hands over it to make sure you didn't miss any spots. This is your shade.

6. Flip the shade over, front side down. There will be half-inch fabric flaps on each side; iron these so they are folded over to the back. Use hot glue to secure them in place. Flip the shade over and hot-glue the fringe along the bottom. Now hot-glue the tassel rope over the fringe of the seam, making sure the tassel hangs from the center. Assemble and install hardware according to package directions and hang.

Tips: Always measure twice and cut once. It will be a sad day in crafty history if you invest in some gorgeous fabric, only to cut it to the wrong size! If your shade ripples after you hang it, it means it was not fused thoroughly. Take it down and re-iron (you don't have to remove the hardware).

❋❋❋❋Take It to the Next Level!❋❋❋❋

✢ Create a modern modular effect by using various textures of fabrics that are in the same color family.

✢ Instead of fusing fabric, buy a large piece of primed canvas and paint a shade.

✢ To add more "pop" to patterned fabric, embellish it with small motifs using glitter squeeze paint.

Clearly Cool Canister Set

VINTAGE COOKING ADS ARE A SLICK WAY TO ADD CULTURE AND A DASH OF WHIMSY TO YOUR KITCHEN DÉCOR. THESE PRINTED DECALS ARE A SNAP TO PUT TOGETHER AND ARE AN ULTRA-cool way to spice up accessories from planters to trivets to windows.

Supplies

Assorted glass canisters with tight rubber seals

1 package of window decal transfer sheets

Assorted images from vintage Latin American food ads, postcards, images cut from calendars, etc.

Make it

1. Measure the surface of the area where you want to apply the decal so you know how much to reduce or enlarge your photos. Insert the window decal sheet in your computer printer and print the images.
2. Cut out the images and apply them to the jars.
3. If desired, embellish the lids with jute, permanent glass paint, or glued-on gems or beads. Let dry.

Tips: The jars look best when filled with white ingredients such as flour, sugar, powdered creamer, or pancake mix. If you want to fill the canisters with darker items, use white ceramic containers. For a permanent application, use Lazertran sheets. You must have the images printed from a laser color copier, and then soak the image in water for a few minutes and apply it to the canister. Rub your fingers over it to remove any bumps. Let dry and seal with polyurethane varnish.

Take It to the Next Level!

✳ These decals are addicting! Use real-life images of flowers or colorful insects and apply them to small square mirrors, windows, or any other glasslike surface.

✳ Look on eBay for collectable retro photos, or visit a local import grocery store, or use current food labels.

Viva Villa! Coffee Coasters

I LOVE MEXICAN *NOVELA* COMICS. THE MELODRAMATIC STORY LINES AND THE RICH ILLUSTRATIONS DO MORE THAN OFFER A GOOD READ. THEY ALSO GENERATE A WEALTH OF DESIGN OPPORTUNITIES. I think it's almost a crime to leave them intact. So next time you are at the import store, pick up two copies: one to read and one to cut up and make into a set of glossy tile coasters.

Supplies

4 ceramic tiles, 4 by 4 inches each

1 *Viva Villa!* Mexican comic book, or any images you prefer

Assorted paints, liner brush, cup of water, paper towel

Loose micro glitter, micro foil stars

White craft glue

1 small box of resin, cup, chopstick, skinny drinking straw

Wax paper

Small wood checkers

E6000 adhesive

Paper mask, thin plastic gloves

Make it

1. Cut out the images to go on the tiles. Use the white craft glue to attach them in place. Squirt a bit of glue on your finger and rub it over the image. The glue will act as a sealant for the picture. Let dry.

2. Dab a glob of paint with your fingertip and glide it over the edges of the coasters to create the look of trim. Let dry. Dip the liner brush in the paint and outline the pictures. Work on one side at a time and, while the paint is still wet, sprinkle on the glitter. Tap the excess off on a piece of typing paper so you can pour it back into the bottle. Use the chopstick to dab little spots of glue and apply the gold micro stars. Let dry.

3. Prepare a smooth table with sheets of wax paper.

4. Working outdoors or in a well-ventilated area, mix the resin according to package directions. Pour a dollop on one coaster and, wearing the gloves, use your finger to move the resin around on the surface, making sure it is completely covered. Wipe away any excess from the edges so it won't drip. Set the tiles

on the wax paper and look for air bubbles. If you see any, pop them by blowing on them with the straw. Let cure for 24 hours.

5. Remove the coasters from the wax paper, flip them over, and glue on the wood checker pieces with the E6000. Paint as desired.

Tips: Always wear a paper mask when doing this project to avoid inhaling fumes. Follow resin-mixing directions as exactly as you can: otherwise it won't cure and your work will be ruined. It's best to let your coasters cure in a garage or laundry room, rather than outside on a patio where annoying creatures like gnats and flies can land—and die—on them. If you have overage that has cured, remove it with heavy-duty scissors or sandpaper. Don't get worried if your resin mixture looks cloudy at first; it usually clears up.

✳✳✳✳Take It to the Next Level!✳✳✳✳

✤ Once you become a resin master, just think of all the fabulous decorations you can make for your home! You can use the above method to decorate patio tables, tea trays, chairs, and *más, más, más!*

✤ Make other coasters by taking shallow candle dishes or flowerpot saucers and layering the bottom with small objects. Pour the resin over and they will look "underneath."

✤ Apply resin to fabric crafts for a dimensional look, or to decorated dominoes.

Add *Sabor* to Your Kitchen Décor

Chili peppers on potholders are cute but clichéd. Pretend your kitchen is going to be used as the set of a funky new prime-time sitcom. Toss out the old and craft in the new with these ideas.

* Decorate a set of dessert plates with bake-on ceramic paint (found at the craft store).
* Buy a set of wood serving spoons and paint them with bright acrylics. Add a layer of polyurethane varnish.
* Buy some memory wire and string chunky glass beads to make classy napkin rings.
* Fill a flowerpot with snipped red roses.
* Take cloth placemats and add fringe on the ends.
* Use imported tins to hold small items.
* Paint your kitchen cabinets in bright colors and add new silver hardware.
* Glue a sawtooth picture hanger to the back of a vintage Mexican serving tray to hang on the wall.
* Buy a blank canvas floorcloth from the craft store and paint and varnish it in big, bold squares.
* Buy vintage dishtowels on eBay; sew them together to make seat covers for folding chairs.

Spray-Painted Shoes

It was the first week of spring, which meant it was time to take my then nine-year-old daughter, Maya, shopping for her annual collection of flip-flops. While she mulled over glittered jellies and beaded slings at the shoe store, I took a peek in my neck of the woods: the size 10W area.

I sifted through boxes upon boxes of ugly clodhoppers until I came across a cute pair of slide-on heels. Not only were they perfect for work, but they were size 9W *and* they fit. I tried them on and giggled in delight when I noticed how the long heel magically extended my legs for an overall slimming effect. There was a teeny glitch though—the shoes were brown instead of my mandatory black.

"Hmmmm, I bet a bit of black spray paint will do the trick" I thought. I figured since they were only $16.99, if the paint job failed, I could just donate them to Goodwill, no sweat.

Later that night, I donned plastic gloves and entered the garage, where there is always black spray paint in stock. I took my new shiny brown shoes, which I loved more with each minute that went by, and I meticulously taped off the heels and the soles. I held each one up and sprayed on an even coat of paint. I let them dry, and then re-applied a heavy second coat, followed by a third.

The next morning I jumped out of bed, excited to shower and dress for work so I could wear my new size 9 shoes that would transform my chunky body into that of Penélope Cruz. I applied my Velvet Vamp red lipstick, spritzed on perfume, inserted my earrings, and skipped to the garage for my new-fangled slide-ons.

I marveled at their beauty—they were a rich, glossy tone of ebony. I slid them on like Cinderella, and swirled my way into the kitchen. The house smelled of bacon, as Patrick was making breakfast. I stopped and posed, like a mod model from a 1960s Simplicity sewing manual. I raised my chin and bragged of my cleverness.

"No wonder they call me Crafty Chica! Look what I did to these shoes!" I beamed.

"You spray-painted your shoes? I don't think that's such a good idea," Patrick said as he shook his head and inserted bread slices into the toaster. "Professional shoe dye exists for a reason, *mujer*."

"WhatEVER, killjoy!" I said just before I downed my espresso and left for the day. I had a new pep in my step and I wanted the world to notice. A couple hours later, I strutted across the newsroom to the mailroom.

"*Ooooo,* sharp shoes, Kath," said a co-worker.

"Thanks!" I replied. My internal dialogue convinced me that I was on to something big. I did a quick mental inventory of all my black shoes to see which ones could use a bit of "freshening" up. I had plenty of spray paint!

Afterwards, I went with my sister Theresa to lunch. We walked a few blocks for healthy salads. I had new shoes, a good-girl lunch, and a brisk walk. Life was perfect! I returned to my office building and entered the elevator. Joining me was a group of couture co-workers. They looked like gilded supermodels—perfect bods, the latest ensembles from *InStyle* magazine, and combined they reeked of delicious

❝'You spray-painted your shoes? I don't think that's such a good idea. . . . Professional shoe dye exists for a reason, *mujer.*'❞

flower bouquets and expensive fruit salad perfume. "Back to reality," I thought. "New shoes or not, I'm Frumpy Housewife again."

"Wow, those are really neat shoes!" one of them said.

"Hey, they *are* cool!" another glam girl added. "They're... like... two-tone."

I wanted to see these fancy shoes. I sipped from the straw in my ice tea and craned my neck downward to see what all the fuss was about.

And then I saw my feet. My straw flicked out of my mouth because my jaw dropped. I was the one with two-tone shoes! I'm talking black *and* brown splotches. My super-fabulous spray paint peeled off in all kinds of crazy, curly directions. And that was after only half a day!

"La, LA, la..." I thought, as I stood there, posing in my best "Yeah, I bought the shoes this way" Angelina Jolie stance. Beads of sweat gathered at the edge of my scalp, ready to begin their race down my forehead as I waited for the doors to open on my floor. "Please God, *please* don't let them ask me anything else about my shoes," I prayed. "Don't let them ask me where I got them, or if they could take a closer look at them. And please let them have been serious about thinking they were hip shoes, and not just be taunting me like the evil blonde chick in *Mean Girls*..."

Ding! The elevator bell rang for my floor. I waited until the ladies filtered out. In the meantime, I wondered how long my shoes had been in that condition. Was it just after lunch,

> **"** 'Hey, they *are* cool!' another glam girl added. 'They're... like... two-tone.' **"**

thanks to the brisk walk? I never made it back to my desk. I made a U-turn and went home. I hid the shoes from Patrick.

From that moment on, I vowed to the crafty gods that I would never again use spray paint so carelessly. It's a powerful tool, but dangerous if put in the wrong situation. I respect that.

As for the shoes, I gave them to Goodwill.

> **"From that moment on, I vowed to the crafty gods that I would never again use spray paint so carelessly. It's a powerful tool, but dangerous if put in the wrong situation. I respect that."**

Crafty Chica's Lesson Learned: Do not spray-paint your shoes and wear them out in public (unless you are a supermodel and need them for a photo shoot). If something seems too good to be true, it probably is. And I don't feel bad about this experience; I'm in good company. Months later, I saw Lara Flynn Boyle on Oprah. She admitted that she had once used gold spray paint on her shoes, right before a red carpet event. And just like me, it was a move she would later regret. The gold paint came off on her legs while she was posing for photographers!

CHAPTER

4

La
DIVA
FASHIONISTA

No matter what your preference, there is a fashion designer out there to match. Every city has an area of trendy boutiques that feature emerging styles, and it's up to you to check it out. But what if you don't have the time or the cash to spend? Hey, I'm right there with you, girl. Take matters in your own hands and be your own designer and stylist. Pinch a little bit of this, and a dash of that, put them in your crafty blender, and see what comes out. Here's a head start for you.

Frida-Inspired Necklace and Earrings

AS A HUMAN, A WOMAN, AN ARTIST, A MEXICAN, AND ALL-AROUND FASCINATING PERSON, FRIDA KAHLO IS AN INSPIRATION TO US CREATIVE TYPES. AND HER DISTINCT TASTE IN CLOTHING AND jewelry is almost as captivating as her artwork. Combos of embroidered blouses, thick rings, and flower- and ribbon-adorned hair can be spotted in modern fashion. My Frida favorite? The necklace. Any necklace. No matter which picture you see of her, she is always decked out in bold, chunky pieces that make a statement. Just like this heavy coral picture necklace, created in honor of her.

Supplies

2 strands of .010 Soft Flex wire, each 18 inches long

1 strand of chunky coral beads

8 medium turquoise beads

2 silver bell caps

2 crimp beads

1 necklace clasp

3 jump rings

1 wood disc, 1½ inches in diameter

1 Frida picture, 1½ inches

White craft glue

Water-based varnish

Black acrylic paint, brush

Needle-nose pliers

Handheld drill or Dremel tool

Make it

1. Paint the wood disc black, let dry, and then glue the picture of Frida to it. Trim any paper that extends over the sides. Paint on a layer of varnish and let dry. This is your Frida pendant. Using the drill or Dremel tool, make a hole at the top of the pendant. Set aside.

2. Now you will start to build the necklace, but first you need to add a crimp bead at the beginning and end of the wire strands. Crimp beads will "anchor" the wire so your necklace will be extra-sturdy. For the first crimp bead: Take the two strands (for double the support because the beads are heavy) of soft flex wire and pinch them together at one end, letting a half inch stick out above your fingertips. Slide on a crimp bead over these two extended strands. Fold over the ends of the strands and thread them back down through the crimp bead so you have a "loop" at the end. Use the needlenose pliers to squeeze and flatten the crimp bead in place.

3. Slide on a bell cap so it is snug against the crimp bead. Now add the beads (three red, one turquoise, two red, one turquoise). Stop when you have two inches of wire left. Slide on the other bell cap.

4. Now for the second crimp bead. This will secure the other end of your necklace. Slide on the crimp bead, fold the end of the double wire strands over, thread them through the crimp bead, and, again, use the needlenose pliers to squeeze and flatten it in place.

5. You will now have two "loops" at each end of the necklace. Add a jump ring to each one. The necklace clasp will come in two pieces. Add one piece to each jump ring. Lay your necklace on a flat surface, find the center and use the third jump ring to attach the Frida pendant.

Tips: If you don't feel comfortable "winging it," buy a bead board at the local craft store. This is a board that allows you to arrange your beads in advance to see what the necklace will look like. Chunky coral and turquoise beads can be found at local beading shops. For a true Frida look, stick with thick silver findings.

❊❊❊❊**Take It to the Next Level!**❊❊❊❊

✤ Buy extra beads and make a bracelet to match.

✤ To make earrings, simply purchase a couple of small wood pieces at the craft store, glue on the pictures, drill a hole at the top, and add jump rings and fishhook earrings.

crystal bead in place. Bring the needle up through the center of one flower, string double-cone bead and pass needle back through flower center; repeat several more times to secure bead. Repeat for each flower.

Tips: Work under good lighting. If you don't know how to crochet, but want to make this project quick, buy crocheted flowers from the craft store and skip to Step 4.

❊❊❊❊Take It to the Next Level!❊❊❊❊

✦ Arrange flowers in a scattered pattern across undershirt. Hand-sew to undershirt. Next, take a few single beads and scatter among flowers; sew to attach. The extra beads will catch the light for more glimmer.

✦ Split center front of undershirt. Finish edges by slightly turning under the edge and sew by hand with matching thread. Measure neck opening from shoulder to shoulder, across front of shirt. Purchase enough decorative trim for neck opening. Sew in place by hand.

✦ Attach varying lengths of silk ribbon when applying the flowers to the neckline for a more flirty finish.

How to Take Your Clothing from Boring to *Bueno!*

Put this book down and look at the clothes in your closet, and then come back. See anything that made you feel daring, edgy, or colorful? If not, read on. You don't have to skip your daily mochas just to be able to revitalize your clothing options. Life is too short to wear the same mix-and-match combinations. Spice it up with some smart-girl rearranging. Try these makeover musings on for size.

✳ **Visit secondhand stores, swap meets, and flea markets for one mission: vintage costume jewelry and accessories!** Especially brooches. Cluster them on a lapel, attach singles to barrette blanks or cuff bracelets. Pick up retro earrings to clip on shoes, handbags, or even a chain to make a funky necklace. If you like the feeling, try out some vintage clothing outfits as well.

✳ **Add scarves.** If you live in a world of monotone separates and power suits, punch them up by tying a silky scarf around your neck or hair. If you're into jeans or trousers, use one as a belt. They also make spiffy bracelets.

✳ **Stock up on blank blouses and embellish them.** Spend a Saturday afternoon watching chick flicks and altering a spaghetti-strap V-neck by sewing beads along the top, embroidering small flowers, or gluing exotic trim on the hem.

✳ **Organize your jewelry and find a place to hang it in view.** The more you look at it, the more ways you'll think about how you can wear it.

✳ **Make a pair of crazy jeans.** Choose one pair of jeans and use a bleach pen (found at grocery stores in the laundry department) to draw all over them. Soak them in fabric dye, or have your friends sign them with a Sharpie pen. Embroider on them, rip them, add patches, etc. Wear them when you are gardening, crafting or lounging, just because.

✳ **Give new life to an old handbag.** OK, I'm not talking about the $700 Fendi bag you got for Christmas; leave that one alone, *por favor.* I'm talking about your standard solid-color clutch or printed beach tote. Pull out the paints and add some vibrancy. Decoupage an image in the center and glue tiny crystals around it. Stencil your initial or favorite phrase. If using a printed bag, enhance the design with glitter. If you don't have spare purses, visit the thrift store.

True Love Always

From the first day I met Patrick, I knew I would spend the rest of my life with him. It took a while for *him* to realize it, but the bottom line is, he did. And I remember the day.

It was a year and a half before we were married. I was managing his *reggae en español* band and we had a Memorial Day gig in Rocky Point, Mexico. The first day, he wore his favorite green, yellow, and red headband that some famous reggae star had given him. It was very windy that weekend, and Patrick offered it to me to restrain my wild curly locks. I accepted and took this gesture as his secret code of "Yes, I am in love with you too." I put the headband on and didn't remove it for the rest of the weekend.

Because it was a holiday, Rocky Point was crawling with drunken college kids that paid no mind to any kind of personal hygiene. When the last morning arrived, the band members loaded up the equipment in our vehicle—an unconditioned food delivery truck that Patrick's dad had lent us. Aside from the front two seats, the truck was empty. Most of us had to sit in the hot steel box the way up and back. But the truck was free for us to use, and we liked that.

I wanted to freshen up before we left. I went into the nearest bathroom and was disgusted by its condition. It hadn't been cleaned in days and stank worse than a chicken farm. I tiptoed through the water on the floor to reach the faucet.

I took off the headband to splash water on my face, but I must have done it too fast because Patrick's beloved head-band flew off my fingers and landed inside the toilet that had not been flushed.

> ❝ I took off the headband to splash water on my face, but I must have done it too fast because Patrick's beloved head-band flew off my fingers and landed inside the toilet that had not been flushed. ❞

There was no way I could go back to the truck and say to my future betrothed, "Sorry, my love, I dropped your favorite headband in the toilet!" What would Patrick say? I plugged my nose and peeked at the damage. The headband was still dry: it appeared to just be resting on the side of the bowl. So I picked up a comb and carefully fished it out. I dropped it in the sink, squirted soap on it, and used the comb to "scrub" it until it lathered. I was in a panic and jumped when I heard Patrick scream at me.

"Kathy! Come on, we're waiting for you!" he yelled from the truck outside. I grabbed the one unused paper towel in the room, blotted the headband, and ran to the truck.

"Hey, gimme my headband back, I need it now, it's going to be a hot ride home," Patrick demanded.

"Here ya go!" I said as I tossed it to him. I jumped in the truck and chewed on my nails, as if I had nothing better to do. Patrick put on the headband, snapped it in place on his sweaty forehead, and climbed on the truck.

I thought I was off the hook. But an hour into the drive, I noticed a faint dirty diaper smell.

"Oh no...," I thought.

As each minute passed, the stench grew stronger. What made it worse was that it was May in Arizona, and the heat was evil. So evil that I couldn't tell if it was just in my paranoid head or if the headband was coming back to haunt me, like a ghost with unfinished business. It wasn't my imagination. Soon, all the band members were eyeballing each other as if to say, "Did you have an accident and not tell us?"

“ I thought I was off the hook. But an hour into the drive, I noticed a faint dirty diaper smell.

'Oh no...,' I thought. ”

The smell was beyond unbearable. I wanted to gag, but I didn't want to draw attention to myself. Still, no one said anything out loud.

Finally, Patrick did.

"What is that *smell*?!"

The band members chimed in unison—"I don't know, man! I didn't do it! Where can it be coming from? Did anyone bring food back? Did someone fart?"

Patrick sniffed and sniffed around the air like a hound dog detective. His head rotated in a large circle with more mini-sniffs. He stopped, but his eyes darted around the truck. Then he looked down, sniffed, looked up, and sniffed again. He ripped off the headband and yelled, "It's *ME*!"

I scrunched my knees up to my chest and buried my head.

"*Kathy!* What did you do to my headband?"

I caved. "I'm sorry! It fell in the toilet back there and I fished it out and tried to wash it but I guess it didn't work very good! I know the famous reggae guy gave it to you and I didn't want you to get mad, so I didn't tell you! I thought it was clean!"

No one said a word, but the bass player/driver pulled the truck over so Patrick could dispose of the caca-infested accessory and wash his head. The remainder of the trip I had to listen to the band lecture me on the dangers of germs. What *ever!* It was a simple, honest mistake made out of *puro amor para mi hombre* (pure love for my man).

So how did I know he loved me? He was only mad for the next couple hours. When he dropped me off at my house,

> **The smell was beyond unbearable. I wanted to gag, but I didn't want to draw attention to myself. Still, no one said anything out loud.**

he smiled and gave me a big bear hug. He lifted my chin, laughed, and said, "Girl, you are something else!" My stomach did the flip-flop thingy and I promised to crochet him a new red, yellow, and green headband. I could tell he was secretly in love with me. I was right because after we got married he admitted it. Little did he know that the headband story was a sign of things to come....

My stomach did the flip-flop thingy and I promised to crochet him a new red, yellow, and green headband.

Crafty Chica's Lesson Learned: Love is like a craft project. The glitter will give you goose bumps and that glue-gun burn will leave a scar. But there is no way to brag about the result unless you experience both pleasure and pain.

CHAPTER

5

Te

AMO

Whether you're married or still looking, there's always room for a little action in the romance department. I can't guarantee these ideas will bring Carlos Ponce to your front door, but I do know they will make the mating dance all the more action-packed. Now go get sexy, fire up the candles, and spin the Franco De Vita CD.

There's a lot of work to be done!

Love Letters Pocket Book

❦❦

THE INTRIGUING ASPECT OF ROMANCE IS THAT IT'S SECRETIVE. NO ONE BUT YOU AND YOUR SIGNIFICANT OTHER KNOW THE INS AND OUTS OF EACH OTHER'S BODY, MIND, AND SOUL. INNOCENT little objects like handwritten notes or pictures make for lifelong mementos, and this book is a way to keep all those tiny tidbits sacred and private. Don't have a date, much less a partner? Make this book anyway. Just doing it will send a message out to the universe that you are ready and available.

Supplies

COVER A: 2 pieces of pattered paper, 5 by 7 inches each

COVER B: 2 pieces of thin cardboard, 3½ by 5½ inches each

COVER C: 2 pieces of patterned paper, 3¼ by 5¼ inches each

1 piece of fabric, 3½ inches square (for binding the book)

1 piece of card stock, 3¼ by 8 inches

3 pieces of patterned paper, 5½ by 6½ inches each

Envelope pattern (page 184)

3 pieces of patterned paper, 3 by 5 inches each

Scissors, ruler, pencil

Glue stick, E6000 adhesive

Metal tag for cover

Assorted pictures to glue inside the book

✳ Make it ✳

1. Make the front and back cover:
   * Take one of the COVER A pieces of paper, flip it over (front side down), and run the glue stick over the *entire* area.
   * Take one of the pieces of COVER B and lay it in the center of COVER A. Rub your fist over it firmly, so it will bond.

* There will be paper flaps from COVER A that extend beyond COVER B. Fold these over and press in place. Smooth out any bubbles with your fingers. Repeat for the other cover. You will have two paper-covered pieces of cardboard.

2. Make the inside components:

* Take the piece of card stock, lay it vertically, and mark off one-inch hash marks all the way down until you have seven of them.
* Create sharp accordion folds on each hash mark, so you end up with an accordion-folded piece of card stock. This is the foundation to hold the envelopes for your book.
* Now attach the accordion-folded card stock to the covers by applying glue stick to the left outer flap, and pressing it along the right side of one of the covers. Rub in place to secure and make sure the ends line up straight. Now repeat by applying glue stick to the outer flap on the right side of the accordion-folded card stock and press it in place along the inner left edge of the other cover of the book. This will make the basic book.
* Add the lining to the inside covers. Take COVER C, flip it over (front side down), and apply glue stick over the entire area. Attach this to the inside of each cover, to serve as the inner lining.

3. Make the envelopes:

* Using the envelope template on page 184, trace it onto one of the pieces of the 5½ by 6½ inch paper: repeat for other papers until you have three. Cut out the shape. Following the lines on the template, fold the envelope, and use the glue stick to secure the bottom and back flap. Repeat until you have made three envelopes.
* Attach the envelopes to the accordion folds. Think of the accordion folds as "hills" (up fold) and "valleys" (down fold). Open the book and line up one of the envelopes lengthwise so the back's bottom meets the "hill." Glue and press in place. Repeat for other envelopes.

4. Use the remaining pieces of paper to cut out tags that will fit in the envelopes. If desired, punch a hole at the top and tie on loose fibers, ribbons, or yarns. Use the glue stick to add photos to each of the pages. Insert tags in envelopes.

5. Close the book and rub your palm over it to make it nice and flat. Now attach the binding. Fold the fabric 1½ inches on one side and repeat for the other side. This will create a half-inch spine. Rub glue stick

on both the inner flaps and slide it over the left side of the book. Smooth out any bumps or bubbles. Decorate the metal tag as desired and use the E6000 to set in place. Insert love letters and pictures in pockets, or write a love poem on each tag.

Tips: For sharper creases, use a bone folder and rub it over your folds. For straighter cuts, use a paper cutter. Both items can be found at local scrapbook stores. Be creative with your papers—use wrapping paper, butcher paper, or even the inside of a brown paper bag. And it's OK if your papers don't line up right: it makes the book look funkier!

✳✳✳✳✳Take It to the Next Level!✳✳✳✳✳

✢ Create several books like this to use as bridesmaids' gifts.

✢ Make a new book for each anniversary, or for special holidays.

✢ Simply increase or decrease the measurements to make the same book in a different size.

White on White Viva el Amor! Shrine

THIS IS AN ASSEMBLAGE MEMORY BOX I IMPROVISED ON BEHALF OF MY NANA AND TATA, WHO HAD BEEN MARRIED FOR DECADES. MY DAD COPIED A PICTURE OF THEM FROM THE 1940S, AND I loved it too much to just put it in a frame. Everything in this love shrine relates to their personalities—as individuals, as well as a couple. I tinted all the components white in honor of their pure spirits and love for each other. I display it in the family room because it makes me feel like they are sending their happy blessings my way. Keep in mind that this project will vary from person to person because the memory items are all different. But here is how I made mine.

Supplies

1 wood box with door

Triangular piece of wood or cardboard

Photo of a couple in love

Water-based acrylic paints, white and silver

Vintage dictionary pages

1 mini-*nicho* (small window box)

1 small doily

Various *milagros* and medals

Assorted card stocks and patterned papers

Assorted embellishments and found objects: ticket stubs from dates, love notes, newspaper clippings, etc.

Stickers, images, old postage stamps

Fringe, trims

Rub-on letters

Ivory lace

Silver tape

Sandpaper

Assorted glues: hot glue, E6000 adhesive, glue stick

Paintbrush, cup of water

Fake flowers

Small personal objects

Make it

1. Squeeze some white paint out, dip the brush in the water and then in the paint, and coat the triangular wood or cardboard. The idea is to make the shrine looked weathered and aged, and this "whitewash" will achieve that effect. Let dry. Add a thin line of E6000 along the top ridge of the box and set the triangle on top. Hold it in place and add a line of hot glue from behind to secure it until the E6000 dries. Dip the brush in the water and then in the paint and thinly cover the box inside and out. Let dry. Rub the sandpaper over the box to make the edges look worn.

2. Open the door to the box to work on the inside area. Now you are going to build the assemblage working from back to front. Start by layering the inner walls of the box with the patterned paper. Affix the doily to the center. Cut the picture of the couple and place it inside the *nicho*. Use E6000 to affix the *nicho* to the center of the doily.

3. Add other items around the area. When you finish, move on to the inside of the door. First apply the paper pieces, such as ticket stubs and newspaper clippings. Let dry and then add a light coat of white paint. Use a coin to apply rub-on letters to spell out the name of the couple. Set the box aside to let everything dry.

4. Decorate the front of the box in the same way. After applying the images, add a light coat of watered-down white paint to make it look like the inside of the box. Use the trims, lace, or fringe to go around the borders of the door. Let dry.

5. Apply silver tape to the top edges of the triangle.

Tips: Visit local import shops to find small items or look on eBay. If gluing heavy objects, first use E6000 and then a dab of hot glue to hold it in place until the E6000 cures. Never use original photos; always make copies. Use curvy scissors on papers to add more shape.

KATHY CANO MURILLO

❋❋❋❋Take It to the Next Level!❋❋❋❋

✣ Make a box not only for you and your *amor,* but also for your parents, a friend, grandparents, etc.

✣ Even if you don't have a *novio,* you can still make a box dedicated to love. Who knows? It could bring you good luck!

✣ Go with other monochromatic color schemes such as red on red, gold on gold, black on black.

✣ Cover the whole box in Spanish love poems or racy comic photo *novelas.*

Potions for Pasión

O N A HOT DATE, DINNER IS SWELL, BUT DESSERT IS DIVINE—ESPECIALLY IF IT COMES IN A JAR AC-COMPANIED WITH A PAINTBRUSH! IF YOU LOVE TO WINE AND DINE ON THE SULTRY SIDE, INVITE your guy over and dig in, sister. Here are three delectable dishes to use in the bath and bedroom. Oh. Don't forget to take the phone off the hook…

AZTEC BODY FONDUE

(MAKES ¼ CUP)

Supplies

2½ tablespoons agave nectar	Candy-flavored oil (optional),
½ tablespoon grapeseed oil	20 drops of raspberry or
1 tablespoon cocoa powder	10 drops of mint

Make it

1. Combine agave nectar and grapeseed oil in a small microwave-safe bowl or Pyrex measuring cup. Heat on high for 6–10 seconds, till slightly warm. Do not overheat! Stir mixture well.

2. Use a flour sifter or mesh strainer to sift cocoa powder to remove any lumps. Add cocoa powder to mixture and continue stirring until completely smooth, using a spoon or small whisk. If using candy-flavored oil, add now.

3. Use it right out of the bowl if you can't wait. Otherwise, store it in a glass jar with a lid with a rubber seal. Stir before use. Apply to body using a clean paintbrush (or fingers). Remove by washing off with warm water, or by…you know! This mixture isn't only a smoldering way to catch your honey's attention; it will also make your skin soft.

Shelf life: *Unopened in sealed jar, three months. Once you open it, use immediately.*

BAÑO DE LECHE (MILK BATH)

(MAKES 1 CUP, 2–4 BATHS)

Supplies

½ cup milk powder

⅓ cup baking soda

⅛ cup arrowroot powder

¼ teaspoon grapeseed oil

½ teaspoon ginger powder
and/or 12 drops of
mint-flavored oil
(optional)

Make it

1. Mix dry ingredients in bowl. Sprinkle grapeseed oil and flavored oil over dry ingredients. Stir to combine.
2. Sift mixture into another bowl using a flour sifter or a mesh strainer to remove all the lumps. Stir sifted mixture, then sift and stir one more time.
3. Package in sterilized jar or food-safe cellophane bag.

How to use it: Add ¼ to ½ cup to warm running bath water, stirring completely to dissolve. You may also first stir it into a cup of warm water before adding to the bath. As with any bath, soaking for longer than 20 minutes will pull moisture from your skin.

Shelf Life: 6–9 months.

baño de leche
(milk bath)

CARAMEL BODY POLISH

(MAKES 8 OUNCES)

Supplies

½ cup dark honey

¼ cup grapeseed oil

¼ cup white cornmeal

1 tablespoon granulated sugar

Candy-flavored oil (optional):
20 drops of mint or 40 drops
of other flavor

Make it

1. Combine honey and grapeseed oil in a microwave-safe bowl or measuring cup. Heat on high for 20 seconds in two 10-second intervals, stirring each time. Do not overheat. Using a spoon or small whisk, stir mixture well and continue to stir occasionally as mixture cools. It will transform into a creamy smooth, caramel-like consistency. Add flavored oil, if desired.

2. Add the cornmeal and sugar to the mixture and stir. Transfer mixture into a sterilized jar and allow to cool completely before adding rubber-sealed lid.

3. Use on hands, feet, or body, but not on face. Massage on damp skin in a gentle, circular motion. Rinse well with warm water. May be left on skin for a few minutes before rinsing for added benefit.

Variation: *For a more gentle polish, replace the cornmeal with sugar. For a stronger polish, use cornmeal in place of the sugar.*

Shelf life: *3 months.*

Tips: If you plan to store these in the bathroom, as opposed to your vanity table, you may want to consider using plastic containers, so they won't be as slippery or breakable. It's a always best to use jars that have a screw-on lid or rubber lip. Cork-top containers are cute but don't provide an airtight seal. We're all clean-freaks, so go ahead and sterilize your jars by thoroughly washing them with hot soapy water. Let dry and then wipe them with a paper towel dabbed in rubbing alcohol. Let dry. Never use products on broken or sensitive skin. Apply with clean fingers or applicator.

✳✳✳✳✳**Take It to the Next Level!**✳✳✳✳✳

✳ Make these as a set and arrange them in a basket and give as a wedding gift.

✳ Create your own "line" of products by designing labels on your computer, or make a collage and wrap it around the jar.

✳ Use a mirrored tray with glass dessert dishes when using these.

✳ Visit a local beauty supply store to find interesting containers, such as test tubes with screw-top lids and holders. Or, better yet, look for fun spice jars.

Fire Up Your Love Life

Do you ever watch a romantic comedy and at the end, when the couple embraces, you dab your eyes and say, "I want love like that"? Well, the movies aren't always far from reality. You can add the misty-eye element to your romance, but you have to be crafty about it. Whatever your current love-life routine is, cancel it. Wipe it off your brain like it's a dry-erase board. Go back to square one. Start here.

* Write down a list of date ideas on small pieces of paper. Put them in a box. Flip a coin to see which of you will get to draw. Whatever is chosen, make that your date. Last-minute decisions are always more fun!
* Visit a paint-on-pottery or paper arts store and make a craft project for each other. At the end of the session, trade it. Don't forget to add a love message in there, then sign and date it on the back.
* Order a big messy meal and share it—one plate, two forks.
* Get dressed up like Beverly Hills movie stars and go out Latin dancing.
* Get his and her spa treatments together.
* Have a fantasy date. He goes with his friends to a club, and you go with your *amigas.* You end up at the same place. One of you asks the other to dance.
* Plan a second honeymoon, even if you've only been together two months!
* Cook a five-course meal together and then feed it to each other.
* When the two of you are together, leave everything else behind. Don't think or talk about problems, work, friends, or anything else. Make it all about the two of you. Soak up the features on each other's faces, the inflections of voices, etc.

Nana's Eternal Candle

My Nana Jauregui is like no other. She is in her late eighties, but she may as well be eighteen. Even at her age, she knows the value of decent face cream, creamy lipstick, and a slenderizing outfit. She primps and poses in the mirror with the same energy as when she was single and heading out on a Friday night date. Until recently, she was a girl-on-the-go. She drove her car to church, the grocery store, the mall, and to her *comadre*'s house for weekly gabfests. And she did it all using right-hand turns only. She was a sister still doin' it for herself.

That changed when she was released from the hospital after hip replacement surgery. It wasn't just her body that was worn down: so was her spirit. There were weeks of physical therapy, an abundance of medication, and specialists galore. No more hair-blowing-in-the wind car rides down the street for a gallon of skim milk.

From then until now, she has relied on us grandkids to help with errands. These included, but were not limited to, three-hour shopping sessions at the grocery store (for half a basket of items), trips to the post office to mail utility bills (she didn't trust the mailbox), and multiple doctor's appointments for a variety of ailments that I will never understand until I reach that age.

When my turn arrived, I discovered these tasks were less than significant compared to the one she deemed most important: lighting her daily prayer candle at the church. When she recited our itinerary for the day, the candle was at the top of the list, and I told her we would save the best for last. I should have made it first. She was edgy all morning until we pulled into to St. Mark's parking lot. It was time to get down to business.

She sat in the passenger's seat of my gold 4Runner and handed me a $10 check.

"Is this a donation, Nana?" I asked.

"No, it's to pay off my candle debt to the church, so I can light a new one," she explained.

Shows how much I knew. I thought you just went in, lit a candle, and left. Not so. I got my instructions for the mission at hand. I was to go inside the main lobby office, see the clerk and pay off Nana's previous candle debt, and then buy—and light—a new candle. I told Nana not to worry; I'd be right back.

I paid the young receptionist; she thanked me, leaned over in her chair, and dragged out a heavy box from a cabinet. She reached in and pulled out a plain glass prayer candle and led me inside the church.

"Here you go, light it anywhere you like," she said.

I was awestruck. This wasn't like my neighborhood church. There were at least five altars, all with dozens of candles flickering in front of them. The sight sent goose bumps up my arms. It was difficult to choose where to place Nana's candle, because each altar looked equally empowering…so I figured the one nearest to where I was standing would be perfect.

As I walked back to the parking lot and approached the car, she watched with an anxious expression and clutched the purse in her lap as if it were her first time

I was awestruck. This wasn't like my neighborhood church. There were at least five altars, all with dozens of candles flickering in front of them. The sight sent goose bumps up my arms. It was difficult to choose where to place Nana's candle, because each altar looked equally empowering…so I figured the one nearest to where I was standing would be perfect.

flying on an airplane. I opened the driver's side door and she lunged at me.

"Was my other candle still burning, *m'jita*? Did you see it?" she asked.

There was no way to tell which candle was hers among the hundred or so that were there. Each burned for a maximum of eight hours, and it had been several days since her last visit. Unless there had been some divine intervention, I was pretty sure her previous candle was long extinguished. But I couldn't bear to break the news. I didn't want to see her sad.

"Oh yes, Nana! There was just a little left of the wax: luckily we came just in time!"

"Ohhhhh, thank goodness!" she said with a sigh of relief. "And did you put it at the feet of Baby Jesus?"

"Yikes. Actually I thought it was the Virgin of Guadalupe's feet," I thought.

"Yup, no worries, Nana!"

I squirmed as my guardian angel lectured me. "One more fib and you're going straight to the devil's basement."

A curvy smile spread across Nana's radiant face, lifting her rouge-tinted cheeks and adding a sparkle to her eyes. All was well and we went on to have an eventful day. The memory used to make me giggle: now it chokes me up. To her, an eternally lit wick represented hope and promise and I wondered what specific request she had for it. World peace? For my sister to find a wealthy husband?

I was curious so one day I asked her what she prayed for.

"Today I'm praying for little Frankie, his arthritis has been

"The memory used to make me giggle: now it chokes me up. To her, an eternally lit wick represented hope and promise and I wondered what specific request she had for it. World peace? For my sister to find a wealthy husband?"

acting up," she said. "I pray for everything. I pray for my children, and my grandchildren and my great-grandchildren. I pray for you. I pray for all of us so that we are all watched over and protected."

On the way home that day, I went to St. Mark's and lit a candle for Nana. I thought about how, as a devout Catholic, this practice began in her childhood. It didn't stop at church. Inside her home of sixty years, her bedroom sports a shrine built into a wall. It holds all her precious *santitos* (saints) and is trimmed in Christmas lights, family photos of all her loved ones, and a tiny candle that is lit 24/7.

My nana and I are two generations apart, yet when I see her spiritual setup, I feel our connection. I have my own shrines and candles of faith and they look just as ornate as hers. OK, maybe more, because I embellish mine with sequins and glitter. But the intention is the same. And I hope that someday, if I ever have a granddaughter, I'll be around long enough so we can light a candle together.

Crafty Chica's Lesson Learned: Respect your elders. What seems like a small favor can have significant meaning. And candles aren't just for making a room smell fresh. Pick up a blank glass prayer candle at the grocery store and embellish it with a picture, a phrase; make a wish and light it. Hope is a powerful tool for manifesting a dream into reality.

CHAPTER

6

Las

LUMINARIAS

Light is a brilliant and stunning way to add drama to your home, and I'm not talking about a dimmer switch. Just like fabric, paper, and paint, light sources can be tailored to your liking. Mini-lights, candles, and outdoor torches are all marvelous, simple ways to add new depth to a flat atmosphere.

Fantástico Fantasy Paper Lights

LEAVE THE PLASTIC PINK FLAMINGO PATIO LIGHTS FOR YOUR NUTTY NEIGHBOR IN THE TIKI SHIRT AND BIRKENSTOCKS. INSTEAD, USE YOUR SCRAPBOOK PAPER LEFTOVERS TO MAKE THIS FOXY strand of mini-lights. However, be aware that this idea is such a breeze, that you may end up making a set for you, and one for everyone on the block.

Supplies

1 strand of 10 white mini-lights (found at the craft store)

10 slide mounts

10 assorted pieces of patterned paper, color copies of photos, magazine pictures, etc.

1 roll of packing tape

1 roll of thin double-sided tape

Dimensional squeeze paint

Hot glue

Pencil

Scissors

❋Make It❋

1. Spread out the pictures and papers. Take one slide mount and place it over the papers to audition images for which ones will show through the hole. Once you find ten, use the pencil to trace around the outer edges of the slide mount on the paper. Cut out the squares.

2. Cover each square, both sides, with a layer of packing tape. Trim excess.

3. Apply a piece of double-sided tape to the inside lip of the mount, both sides. Peel up the backing from the tape on one side. Carefully set the paper in place, making sure it is centered. Rub the edges with your finger so it bonds with the tape. Peel away backing from the tape on the other side of the mount, and press down firmly so it locks in place. Rub with fingers to secure it. Trim excess paper. Repeat for remaining slide mounts.

4. Test light strand to make sure it works. Apply hot glue to the upper casing of one of the mini-lights. Don't apply it to where the bulb connects (in case one burns out and you need to replace it). Press the slide mount onto the glue and hold down with finger until the glue dries. Try to align all the mounts so they line up even when the strand is hung.

Tips: Always make a color copy of any pictures, especially if using magazine or comic book images, because the other side will shine through when the light is on. Stick with low-watt craft lights that are meant to be embellished.

✳✳✳✳**Take It to the Next Level!**✳✳✳✳

✳ Double the recipe and apply the slide mounts to both sides of the lights, so no matter which direction you look, you will see an image.

✳ For a vintage look, check out flea markets or antique stores to find old-fashioned metal or cardboard mounts, as shown in the picture.

✳ You can also use regular colored paper: just enhance it by applying rubber-stamped images, or just draw on it with a pen!

✳ Create mini-collages in a larger size, reduce them when making color copies, and use them for your lights.

✳ Use pictures of your family for each light, or favorite quotes, Mexican *lotería* cards, etc.

Tin-Trimmed Garden Stakes

Don't you hate it when you go to backyard party and the host has the same décor as you? It's as if you shopped at the same store. The agony! We artists need to work harder to stamp our style in our swanky *casas*. These charming candle stakes are a sure way to do that.

Supplies

1 terra-cotta pot, 4-inch
    diameter
1 wood dowel, half-inch round
1 cheap pair of scissors
1 disposable tin cookie sheet
E6000 glue

Acrylic paints, brush
Embossing tin
Blue painter's tape
Votive candles, or, if using in an
    open tree-free space, pillar
    candles

☀ Make It ☀

1. Cut the rimmed edges off the cookie sheet, leaving a smooth piece of tin. Cut that into one-inch strips. Be daring with your scissors and cut the strips into curvy or wavy designs.

2. Set the pot upside down and apply the E6000 around the brim. Line up one of the strips of tin with the edge of the pot's brim and wrap the tin around until the ends meet. Hold in place with your hands. Apply a piece of blue painter's tape on the ends to keep in place. Let dry for several hours.

3. Hold the dowel to the hole at the bottom of the pot. If the hole is too small, open the scissors, insert one of the blades in the hole, scrape away. Stop and check to see if the dowel fits. **Important:** Do this a little at a time because you don't want the hole to get bigger than the dowel; you want it to fit tight and snug.

4. With the pot upside down on a flat surface, apply E6000 glue generously around the end of the dowel and insert it into the hole at the bottom of the pot, so the dowel is sticking straight up. Do not let the dowel protrude too far down inside the pot, otherwise your candle will wobble when the pot is right-side up. Let the glue cure for 8 to 10 hours.

5. When the glue is dry, paint the pot and the dowel. Let dry. Insert the dowel deep in the ground so it will stand firm.

Tips: During the drying process, if your dowel begins to lean, it means you made the hole too big. You can still save it! Just use packing tape to secure it to the base of the pot, so it will stand and dry straight. Do not paint the pot before you glue on the tin; it will not hold.

❋❋❋❋**Take It to the Next Level!**❋❋❋❋

✢ To mix up the look, instead of tin, decorate the brim with beaded or fabric trim, fringe, mosaic designs, letters, etc.
✢ Fill the pots with small rocks and use to hold tea light candles.
✢ Instead of candles, insert clear plastic cups into the pots and use them to hold snacks at your next party.

Corazón Candles

I LOOK AT THICK PILLAR CANDLES AND I SEE A BLANK CANVAS, WAITING TO BE ADORNED WITH DELI-CATE DESIGNS. ONCE I SPLURGE MY TIME AND LABOR ON ENHANCING THEM, I DON'T DARE BURN them. And that's cool. Candles are plentiful. Pick up some good quality pillars (the kind that don't need to be lit to smell good) and gaudy them up with pictures, fibers, and other objects. My advice? Use them for decoration only.

Supplies

Pillar candle

Tissue paper with *corazón* images, or newsprint

Raffia and/or jute cording

Embossing heat tool

Paper plate

Glue stick

✳ Make It ✳

1. Tear or cut out the image from the tissue or newsprint paper. Apply the glue stick on the back of the image. Set in place on the front of the candle.

2. Hold the candle while resting the bottom on the paper plate. Tilt it at an angle, and run the embossing heat tool over the image in a swirly motion. You will see the candle wax melt and absorb the paper. Keep moving the heat so the wax won't melt too much in one area. There will be drips of wax, but you can even out the look by running the heat on the other areas of the candle.

3. When the image is melted into the candle, let it cool. Embellish by adding cording, etc.

Tips: This project will work only if you use thin paper, such as tissue or newsprint. Never try to use thicker paper because it will melt away too much of the wax from the structure of the candle. If you want to use a thicker paper, sandwich it between two pieces of wax paper, set it on the candle, and then run the heat gun over it. Always work over a paper plate to catch the wax drippings. If you don't care about having a melted look, you can just glue pictures on, but they will most likely peel off.

Safety tip: Never leave lighted candles unattended. If you absolutely *must* burn your decorated candles, make it for a special occasion and put them out when they burn down within an inch of the image.

✳✳✳✳**Take It to the Next Level!**✳✳✳✳
✳ Make candles to commemorate an event by clipping the announcement from the newspaper.
✳ Paint your own designs on tissue paper to use on your candles.
✳ Apply rubber-stamped designs on the newsprint for a contrasting, artsy look.

Use Good Karma to Light Up Your Life

Ever have days when you feel like you're stuck with the short end of the glue stick? Maybe you need to send out some positive vibes. It's that whole "what goes around, comes around" thing. Even if you think it's a bunch of bunk, it doesn't hurt to give sweet surprises to other people. Not only will it make them feel warm and fuzzy inside, you'll feel great too! Think of karma as a positive energy bank account. You always want to make sure it's filled.

* Nip nasty gossip in the bud. Switch the conversation to something nice.
* The next time you have an impulse to pass a judgment, go give that person a compliment instead.
* Make a batch of whimsical magnets or lapel pins and carry them in your purse. When you bump into someone who looks like they need a pick-me-up, give them one!
* Bake cupcakes with fluffy frosting and take them into your job or school.
* Give up an object or favorite piece of clothing that you love but don't use anymore. Donate it to a women's shelter.
* Call an old friend and catch up. Don't talk about yourself; let the conversation be about her.
* Focus on valuing relationships over material objects.
* Mentor a young person or speak to a youth group or classroom.
* Give back to your community. Call your local women's shelter and offer to teach a craft class. If you feel successful in your life, offer to speak at a workshop.
* Practice gratitude and appreciation. Make a list of all the good things in your life. Keep it in your wallet. When you feel cheated, pull out the list and count your blessings.
* Good karma begins with a good thought. If you don't have time to do anything, at least send out encouraging vibes.
* When someone ticks you off, think to yourself, "How does this affect my big picture in life?" Usually it has zero effect. Shrug it off and don't let it ruin your day.
* Give out and never expect anything in return; that way your life will always be filled with pleasant surprises.
* Love yourself. Be proud of what you've accomplished. It will make you an example for others to do the same.

El Cucuys de Maya

If you had the chance to launch a successful worldwide business at the age of eleven, wouldn't you just be all over it, like glitter on a New Year's Eve party hat? I know I would.

My daughter, Maya, thought differently and Mommy had to teach her a lesson. My little missy began making super-cute stuffed felt monsters one fall season. They were such a hit that friends and family began to place orders. Not as many as a Bloomingdale's catalogue, but two or three a month, which was a lot for a preteen. It happened so fast—one day it was a giddy Saturday afternoon time-passer, and the next she was juggling a stack of felt, hand-drawn patterns, a pin cushion, thread, and a bag of googly eyes. Maya is so-so on the sewing machine, and my friend Vanessa had just trapped her finger under her machine's moving needle; I had nightmares about the same horror happening to Maya. So I coached her on the old-school method of hand-stitching. As a result, each monster required at least two hours, but they came out adorable. Patrick and I were thrilled. Maya was so proud of this monster movement that we considered building her a Web page, www.CucuysdeMaya.com, and when you clicked on it, you would hear a ghostly chorus of *"Www-wooooooooo . . ."*

Yeah, we *all* thought Maya was on her way to an early career in the retail world. A junior Donald Trump of crafts. We envisioned the international launch party of *Cucuys de Maya* in toy stores all over the world. We'd buy a mansion, send her and our son, DeAngelo, to an overseas university—or, even better, Patrick and I could go on a trip to Europe!

> **"** Yeah, we *all* thought Maya was on her way to an early career in the retail world. A junior Donald Trump of crafts. We envisioned the international launch party of *Cucuys de Maya* in toy stores all over the world. **"**

But *noooooo* . . .

A week later, *mi'jita* polished off the last order on her list. She tossed the monster on the table, stood up from her chair, and aggressively slashed her little hands in the motion of an "X" across her chest.

"Mommy, this business has closed down! I'm *sick* of making monsters!" she said. That lasted for a couple days. She received a request for three more, and she snatched the cash. In her mind, she had already spent the funds on a new Game Boy cartridge.

"Can you take me to the store, Mommy? It's super-important," she asked one evening.

"Sure, for more felt for the monsters?"

"No way! For the new *That's So Raven* game. I have enough money to buy it now."

"Maya," I said, "you can't buy games until you buy the supplies for the order."

"But then I won't have enough for my game!" she cried.

"Well, then you can't buy it yet."

That last comment sent her over the edge. She didn't want to put in the sweat, but she wanted the payoff. I watched as she switched on her saddest frown and let her oversized eyes fill with tears of frustration.

It didn't faze me. I warned her about the pros and cons of supply and demand when she initially decided to sell the monsters. Now it was time for Mommy Defcon Four and I fired up the life-altering lecture. I reinforced the basics of business. I told her it was a blessing that someone wanted

❝ 'Mommy, this business has closed down! I'm *sick* of making monsters!' ❞

to buy her work, and how a lot of people weren't so lucky. I told her she couldn't make the monsters and be angry at the same time because it defeats the purpose of creating meaningful art. I made it clear that if she agreed to accept an order, she had to fulfill her end of the bargain before she could hit Target's electronics department.

"Do you understand what I'm saying, Maya?" I asked.

"Yes, Mommy. So... can we go get my game now?"

I bit my tongue and smiled. I asked her to please fork over the thirty bucks.

"Maya, my dear. You are now free from your monsters' evil grip. I'll finish up the order. But that means I get to keep the money."

"What?" she said.

"Don't worry about it, sweetie. You're still too little to handle something like this. Maybe when you're older we can revisit this. Until then, if you want to earn money for the *That's So Raven* game, I have some extra chores you can do around the house. In fact, I see some spotty windows winking at you right now."

I kissed her soft pink cheek and walked to the art studio to pull out the sewing machine.

She posed like a statue, astonished. It registered in her fifth-grade brain that the cash was slipping right through her greedy little fingers. She ran after me, tugged on my blouse, fell to her knees, clasped her hands together, and gave me an extreme dose of *la Sad Girl* eyes.

"I'm sorry, Mommy. I really *do* like making monsters. I

> " 'Maya, my dear. You are now free from your monsters' evil grip. I'll finish up the order. But that means I get to keep the money.' "

really, really, really want to make those three monsters, *really* I do. *Please* can I have one more chance? I promise I won't complain."

I responded with a poker face. I love those moments. My little drama queen flipped her eyes to the ceiling, summoned some faux tears (I thought I was the only one that had that ability), looked back at me, and blinked her lids like a wounded poodle.

"*Pleeease, Mommy???*"

"OK, but only if you are 100 percent sure."

We both had a new wind of motivation, and embarked on a guilt-free shopping spree for felt and faux fur. I gave her the $30 and she paid for the supplies at the register. She had enough left over for a book and a package of fluorescent hair scrunchies. We worked together on the monsters, and even made a few extra. I didn't want Maya to spend time on a hobby she hated. But I did want her to finish what she started, and to have the right attitude.

Cucuys de Maya was back in business. But I have yet to book that trip to Europe.

Crafty Chica's Lesson Learned: Be careful what you ask for! If you want to make something to sell, give it a trial period. The quickest way to subtract love from art is to be forced to mass-produce it.

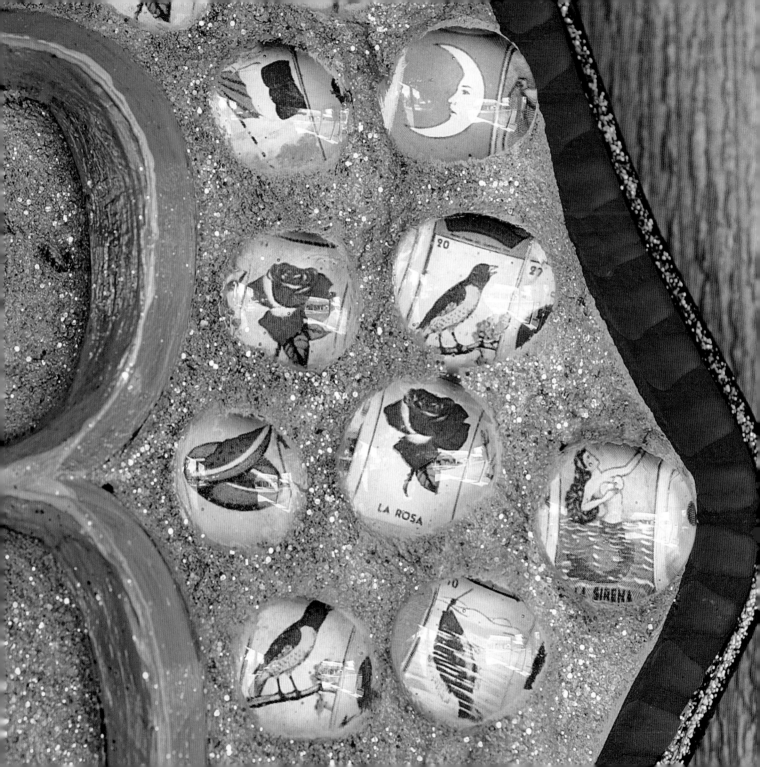

CHAPTER

7

PATIO
PLEASURES

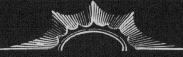

We all have times when we need to escape for a breath of fresh air, but don't have time to leave the house. Agree? Well, that's when the patio becomes our new best friend. Grace it with your craftsmanship and *talento*, and that covered porch will become a mini-sanctuary of tranquillity and harmony. Release your creativity out the doors and windows of your home so that crafty goodness will filter into items such as painted flowerpots, fabric-covered chairs, and radiant wind chimes. And that's just a start. Here are some more ways to add enchantment and excitement to your outer portions.

Flamin' Firepot

WHEN I WAS SETTING UP THE PHOTO SHOOT FOR THIS BOOK WITH CAMERAMAN JOHN SAMORA, I SPOTTED THIS FIREPOT ON HIS BACK PATIO. I COULDN'T BELIEVE WHAT HE TOLD ME HE made it from—a washing machine tub! I couldn't help but beg him for the instructions. Assemble one of these bad boys and your next shindig will be a remarkable one.

Supplies

1 enameled washing machine tub from your local appliance salvage yard

1 premade steel pot stand, 16–18 inches round (available at home improvement stores, plant nurseries, or Mexican import shops)

3 cable clamps, 3/8 inches wide (found at hardware store). These are U-shaped bolts with nuts attached.

6 lock washers for the cable clamps

Electric drill

7/16 inch drill bit

9/16 inch wrench or ratchet

Measuring tape

Felt-tip marker

Hammer

Stout nail

Make It

1. On a level surface, flip the washing machine tub upside down. Flip the pot stand over, and center it on the tub. Use the tape measure to make sure it's centered.

2. Take one of the cable clamps, remove the nuts, and use it as a guide for the holes you're about to drill. Place the bolts at equidistant points around the pot stand and mark the spots where you should drill your holes.

3. Remove the pot stand from the tub. Take the nail and with the hammer, make an indentation in the center of each mark as a starting dimple for the drill bit. Drill out the holes.

4. Replace the pot stand, insert the cable clamps, and carefully slip the lock washers and nuts on the inside of the tub. At this point it's OK to keep them loose.

5. Flip the tub over to its new legs, and adjust it until everything is centered, then tighten the bolts with the wrench or ratchet until snug.

Tips: Keep in mind that when you build a fire, the firepot (being metal) will be *very* hot. Do *not* try to move it or touch it while a fire is burning. Keep in mind that ash and small coals may drop out the bottom. Use caution and common sense as to where you place your firepot. Concrete, bare ground, or bricks are ideal spots. If you place it on your lawn, make sure you have bricks or paving stones beneath, as your lawn can catch fire if you're not careful. Do *not* place it on a wooden deck, do *not* place it under a patio roof, and do *not* try to use it indoors. Do not paint or apply anything to this piece, as the fire's heat will add a rustic aged look to it. Never leave the fire pit unattended. A Weber grill lid or a galvanized trash can lid from your local hardware store fits perfectly on the top and will prevent sparks from flying after you retire from your fire. The trash can lid can be had for $3, and old Webers can sometimes be found at garage sales for $10 or less.

❀❀❀❀**Take It to the Next Level!**❀❀❀❀

✤ If you have a large backyard and are having a big party, make multiple fire pits and place them throughout. Lay down a base of square patio tiles as a foundation to set each one upon.

✤ Instead of making it a fire pit, use it as a planter for your yard.

DON'T YOU EVER YEARN TO SAY "MY HOUSE IS EASY TO FIND, JUST LOOK FOR THE PICTURE MARBLE MOSAIC ADDRESS SIGN"? OK, MAYBE YOU NEVER THOUGHT OF THAT, BUT NOW THE SEED IS planted. If you are going to spend all that time to dress up the inside of your walls, you may as well do the same for the outside.

Supplies

1 wood plaque, 12 inches (found at craft store)

Wood numbers

2 bags of small flat-back glass pebbles

3–4 sheets of *lotería* playing cards

Glues: E6000 and white craft glue

Charcoal mosaic grout

Assorted water-based acrylic paints

Glitter varnish/sealer

Scissors

Sponge, paper towels, water

Protective gloves

Make It

1. Use E6000 to glue numbers on the plaque; let dry. Base-coat the plaque in desired colors. Let dry.

2. Add a thin layer of the white craft glue to the back of the marbles and set them on top of the *lotería* playing card sheets. The glue will dry clear so the image will show through. Cut out the marbles and trim excess off from the edges. Put on protective gloves, dip your finger in the E6000, and rub the glue around the seam of the marble, where the picture ends. This is to seal it, so when you grout, water will not seep in. Let dry. Use the E6000 to glue the picture marbles all over the plaque, around the numbers. Squeeze them as close together as you can. Let dry.

3. Prepare the grout to the consistency of creamy peanut butter. Wearing the gloves, spread it in between the marbles and numbers. Wipe your finger around the edge of the wood to make it look even. Let it set five minutes and then wipe away the excess with a damp sponge so the marbles emerge. Let sit for 30

minutes and then use a damp paper towel to wipe around the edges of everything and to clean the tops of marbles. Let dry until grout has hardened.

4. The numbers will need touch-ups, so go back over them with paint, and highlight with a lighter shade for more definition. Let dry and then apply a layer of glitter varnish over all the grout. This will also act as a sealer.

5. Add hardware or drill holes in the back to hang.

Tips: If you don't want to go through the mosaic process, just cut up the cards and decoupage them around the numbers and add sealer. If you don't want to use picture marbles, use small, precut colored tiles (found at the craft store).

✳✳✳✳Take It to the Next Level!✳✳✳✳

✢ Thread thick glass beads onto a long piece of wire and attach the ends with screws to the back of the plaque for more of a folk art look.

✢ Go for a bigger statement by using a large piece of pine, instead of the wood plaque.

✢ Instead of house numbers, use letters that spell out your *familia*'s last name.

Wonderfully Worn Flower Fence

Y OU DEDICATED HOURS OF SWEAT, BRUISED KNEES, AND CALLUSED HANDS FOR THAT SCRUMP- TIOUS FLOWERBED. NOW FRAME IT UP WITH A DELIGHTFUL HAND-PAINTED MINI-FENCE. THIS is a project that is best made outside, where you can let nature work its magic on you and your paintbrush. Simply take the hues from *las flores* and use paint colors to match. If you need guidance, look at the bushes, trees, flow-y vines, and leaves around you and let your imagination recreate them on wood.

Supplies

1 wood lawn border

Assorted acrylic paints, white, purple, pink, yellow, and green

Sea sponge, water

Heavy grit sandpaper

Base-coat brush

Fine-liner brush

Make It

1. Paint the entire wood lawn border with one coat of white paint. Let dry and use a damp sea sponge to add accents of the other colors on the inside "criss-cross" area.

2. At the top of the border, in the center, use the fine-liner brush and paint to write your phrase. Add flowers and vines of leaves on the remaining areas of the top and bottom areas. Let dry.

3. Take the sandpaper and rub the lawn border at the edges, tops, and sides—even on top of the paint! You want the wood to show through. Insert in your flowerbed and enjoy.

Tips: If you have trouble with freehand drawing, pick up some stencils at the craft store. However, using your own writing adds a more folk art and primitive look. Always let the paint dry before sanding, otherwise it will smear and ruin the overall look.

✳✳✳✳✳**Take It to the Next Level!**✳✳✳✳✳

✳ Instead of a short phrase, write a favorite inspiring quote.

✳ Make several of these and line them all up to match your garden.

✳ Paint lawn chair furniture and pottery to match.

✳ Use old broken china to make a mosaic design.

Retreat to Your Backyard Sanctuary

One of the joys of traveling is to experience new surroundings. But if you can't get away, go for the next best thing: your backyard. Devote a few weekends to making it a fantasy-like escape, a place to relax, dream, and of course—make art!

* Walk around your yard and look at the potential of all the areas. Choose one area to make into a meditation corner. Put up a cheery tarp, a rug, pillows, and a small chest or end table. You can either add a chair or just lie on the rug.
* Buy a set of raw wood Adirondack chairs. Paint them in a soothing color and add a layer of glitter varnish, so they will glimmer in the sunlight.
* If you don't have time to plant a garden, buy potted plants and insert them in painted pots all over your yard.
* Invite the kids in the family to come over and help you paint river rocks or bricks (found at the home improvement store). Look at each rock and see what the shape reminds you of—a cloud? a ladybug? a bottle of tequila? Draw the design with a pencil and then fill in with paint. Line them up along a walkway, or mix them in with your other rocks.
* Make a batch of mosaic stepping stones and use a chopstick to write in your favorite words. You can find kits at the craft store.
* Paint the ceiling of your outdoor patio like the sky—light blue with soft swirls of white for the clouds.
* String beads on long pieces of fishing line and then tie them to holes on an old bicycle wheel rim. Thread a piece of rope up the center and hang.
* Create a wind chime display. Choose an area of your yard and insert assorted sizes of garden shepherd hooks into the ground. Hang the wind chimes from them.

All about *Día de los Muertos*

There's only one time when partying with the dead makes sense: *Día de los Muertos.* The thought of jovial dancing skeletons appears very cool, but not in a gothic-y morbid sort of way. *Día de los Muertos* is all about giving props to our loved ones who have passed on. Rather than mourn the loss, we say *"Viva!"* to their life not only in this world, but also in the next.

During *Día de los Muertos,* people set up funktified *ofrendas* in their home, complete with layers of decorations, flowers, pictures, food, and special mementos. The idea is to lure loved ones back for one glorious day of pure bliss. The bones of it begin on October 31 by first preparing for the spirits of children to visit on November 1. These angels follow the scent of marigolds and the yummy food their family has set out for them. But even in the afterlife the kids have a curfew. By noon they must return to the spirit world so the adult souls can take their turn until November 2, when they too must head back to the afterlife. Throughout these days, we "flesh heads" honor them with a feast—we eat their favorite meal, sing their favorite ballads, and exchange happy memories. Even though we can't see their bodies, we know their spirits are close by joining in the fun.

This is why the imagery centers on whimsical and often mischievous *calacas* (skeletons). The skeleton suggests that the body may be gone, but the personality is still intact.

The pre-Columbian concept was born more than three thousand years ago at what is now Mexico City. Taking place at the summer harvest festivals, *Día de los Muertos* was

> ❝ The idea is to lure loved ones back for one glorious day of pure bliss. . . . Even though we can't see their bodies, we know their spirits are close by joining in the fun. ❞

> ❝ This is why the imagery centers on whimsical and often mischievous *calacas* (skeletons). The skeleton suggests that the body may be gone, but the personality is still intact. ❞

their way of honoring deceased ancestors. And they were downright serious—using actual skulls in their *ofrendas* to represent life and death. However, the ritual went over as well as a week-old tortilla with the Spaniards. When they invaded the land centuries ago, they didn't only freak, they were appalled; they condemned the practice as sacrilegious and tried to abolished it. The headstrong Aztecs refused. Because they stood firm, *Día de los Muertos* lived on but was moved to early November by the Spanish priests, to coincide with All Soul's Day and All Saint's Day. Hey, a compromise is better than nothing.

These days, the glittery gala is bubbling on both sides of the border with colorful community festivals, art markets, homemade food, and mariachi music. In Mexico the customs vary; in some regions the *ofrenda* is created at the gravesite rather than at home. Americans of all cultures have also come to embrace *Día de los Muertos* in their own signature style. Aside from making artsy altars, some folks write poetry, paint murals, or attend memorial services.

Now it's up to you to find your own way of celebrating your ancestors.

" Now it's up to you to find your own way of celebrating your ancestors. "

CHAPTER

8

DÍA
de los
MUERTOS

Even though *Día de los Muertos* is officially in November, many people celebrate it all year-round. That's because paying tribute to loved ones who have passed on brings comfort. It forces us to remember these people for all they accomplished on earth as well as to accept that their spirits are still with us.

La Femenina Ofrenda

PIECING TOGETHER AN *OFRENDA* (ALTAR) IS A PERSONAL EXPERIENCE. IT'S SOOTHING, EMOTIONAL, AND EMPOWERING ALL AT THE SAME TIME. THE PROCESS IS A LOOSE ONE, SO FEEL FREE TO make your own guidelines. It can be a grouping of a picture, a book, a candle, and a rose, or it can be grandiose, like a sixteen-foot community altar. It all comes down to the message of the person assembling it. This *ofrenda* is an example of a nontraditional altar and it is dedicated to *las mujeres* of *el mundo*.

Supplies

1 wood wall shelf with a back panel or attached frame (found at craft store)

Día de los Muertos picture of woman

Pictures of loved one

Greenery, flowers (faux)

Small tea light candle and holder

Small personal objects or items reflecting female empowerment

1 roll of crepe paper party streamers, orange and yellow

Assorted glues: E6000, hot glue, and white craft glue

Acrylic paint, cranberry

Torn strips from a Spanish newspaper

Medium paintbrushes

Make It

1. Working with one section at a time, apply a thin layer of white craft glue on the wood. Lay down the strips of the newspaper in a random fashion. If edges overlap, add more glue to seal them down. Repeat until entire surface of the altar is covered. Let dry and then apply one coat of the cranberry paint to entire piece. Let dry.

2. Using hot glue, attach leaves to the shelf area. Attach a large flower to the top, in the center, and more greenery as desired.

3. Insert a picture of a *muertos* woman in the frame, or affix it to the back panel of the altar.

4. Set or hang the altar where you want it and then place the personal objects and pictures on the shelf.

Tips: Always use extra care when using candles in an altar. Stick with tea lights and place them in glass candleholders to prevent a possible fire hazard. If the altar is temporary, use fresh marigolds and greenery. For a more traditional look, incorporate sugar skulls, *copal* and *papel picado*.

❋❋❋❋Take It to the Next Level!❋❋❋❋

✤ Make a larger, more ornate altar by using a tabletop as the foundation.

✤ Use smaller wood bases to create an altar for all the women from the past who have inspired you.

✤ For a permanent piece, create a shadowbox using photos and mementos or better yet, try the My Favorite Things Table project on page 25!

A Glossary for *Día de los Muertos*:

Calavera: A skull.

Calaveras: Songs and poems about the festivities.

Calaveritas de azúcar: Skulls made from sugar, that are decorated with colored foils and icing.

Careta: A mask worn by dancers to scare the dead back home at the end of the night.

La Catrina: Artist José Guadalupe Posada's iconic drawing of a wealthy woman in Victorian dress.

Cempazuchitl: Marigold flowers, known as the symbol of death.

Copal: A scented resin used to make incense that is burned at the *ofrenda.*

Pan de los muertos: Sweet bread that is baked in honor of the dead.

Papel picado: Tissue paper banners with scenes that are intricately cut out.

For a Traditional Altar, Leave the Following Items:

Drinks: Because the dead are thirsty after the long journey home.

Food: Make their favorite meal; they will appreciate it!

Lighted candles: So they can warm their hands during the chilly season.

Salt: It is considered the spice of life!

Papel picado: It signifies that the *ofrenda* is a celebration of life.

Mole: It is one of the most popular dishes left at the altar because of its sweetness.

Marigolds and copal: The combination of these scents leaves a trail for the dead to find their way home.

Baby's breath and white orchids: These are for *ofrenda* made for children.

White Chocolate Sugar Skulls

S UGAR SKULLS LOOK SO TEMPTING TO EAT. BUT DON'T DO IT. YOU'LL GET A MAJOR TOOTHACHE. THAT'S BECAUSE, *MI AMOR,* SUGAR SKULLS ARE, WELL, PURE SUGAR. HOWEVER, THERE IS A TASTY twist you can pull off. This recipe still uses the sweet stuff, but in a more edible-friendly way: white chocolate! Not only will you win the Prettiest Sugar Skull award, but you'll also be able to eat your work!

Supplies

1 tray of mini sugar skull molds	1 roll of wax paper
Measuring cup	Assorted tubes of Frosting
1 bag of Wilton white	Doodle or other mini-tubes
chocolate chips	of colored icing
1 microwave-safe mixing bowl	Sugared flowers, edible glitter,
1 mixing spoon or chopstick	candy sprinkles

Make It

1. Put one cup of chips in the bowl. Microwave on high for 15 seconds. Remove and stir. Repeat for 15-second intervals, stirring after each one, until all the chips have melted to a creamy consistency. It's crucial to keep stirring; otherwise the chips will scorch.

2. Spoon the mixture into the molds. Using both hands, lift the tray about six inches from the table and drop it. This will allow the mixture to settle in the grooves of the mold, and it will remove any bubbles. Let cool until firm.

3. Flip the skulls on a sheet of wax paper. Knead the tube of frosting until the contents are of an even consistency. Test by squeezing on paper. If the frosting is watery at the top, remove the lid and stir with a chopstick. Draw eyes, flowers, hearts, or any other desired designs on each skull.

4. Decorate the frosting by pressing in sugar flowers or spinkling on candy glitter. Wrap the finished skulls in small cellophane bags with ties and keep refrigerated until it's time to eat.

Tips: The key to success with this project is to keep stirring the chips when you remove them from the microwave. That way they will melt into each other and create a creamy texture. Visit a local cake-decorating shop to find tiny sugar decorations to use on your skulls.

✳✳✳✳✳Take It to the Next Level!✳✳✳✳✳

✤ Make multicolored skulls by coloring the melting chips (pink, purple, red, green, etc.).

✤ Write the names of your friends on the foreheads of the skulls and pass them out.

✤ Give them as party invitations. Put each one in a small clear bag, tie it with a ribbon, and attach a card with info about the party.

✤ Instead of using small molds, use large full-size skull molds and decorate with larger frosting applicators.

Bandera de Calaca (Skull Banner)

THE PURPOSE OF HANGING SPLASHY BANNERS FOR *DÍA DE LOS MUERTOS* IS TO SHOW THAT THE FESTIVITIES ARE A CELEBRATION, NOT A "MOURN-ABRATION." IT'S BELIEVED THAT THE SOULS OF the dead are hurt if they return and are greeted by weeping relatives. Traditional altars use *papel picado* (Mexican tissue banners) to signify the party, but you can be innovative by using this sassy substitute.

Supplies

1 red cloth napkin with patterned border, 16 by 16 inches

1 Clorox Bleach Pen

1 package of the Creative Iron fusible fabric borders

1 piece of balsa wood, 16 by 4 inches (found at craft store)

8 grommets and grommet tool

Ribbon

Acrylic paints, gold and red

Strand of fringe, 17 inches long

Hot glue

Small handheld drill

Make It

1. Lay the napkin on a large piece of cardboard. Shake the bleach pen and remove the cap from the "fine point" side. Draw a skull, with eyes, nose, and mouth, and make sure the bleach gel is in a thick even line. Add designs or words to the border areas of the napkin if you want. Set it aside for 25–30 minutes until you lift it off the cardboard and see that the design has thoroughly soaked through to the other side of the napkin. When it has, rinse the napkin in warm water, wring out, dry in the dryer, and then iron the wrinkles out so it is flat and crisp.

2. Lay the napkin on the ironing board and position the fusible fabric borders around the edges. Set iron on "cotton" and iron the borders in place.

3. Paint the piece of balsa wood red, decorate it with words and designs, and let it dry. Drill three holes along the bottom (to attach to the napkin) and two along the top (to attach ribbon for hanging). Attach grommets in holes using the grommet tool (see package for directions).

4. Using a hole punch, make three small holes along the top of the napkin, making sure they line up with the holes on the balsa wood. Attach grommets to the napkin holes.

5. Attach the painted piece of balsa wood to the napkin: thread a 3-inch piece of ribbon through the grommets from the bottom of the balsa wood to the top of the napkin.

6. Cut two 8-inch pieces of ribbon and tie one to each hole at the top of the balsa wood. Tie the two ribbon strands together, so the banner can be hung.

7. Run a line of hot glue along the bottom edge of the napkin and apply the top edge of the fringe. Let the fringe extend past each edge, and then flip the piece over and glue the ends in place.

Tips: Practice your skull drawing before you use the bleach pen on the napkin. Don't draw your skull's features too close together because the bleach gel spreads out a bit. The thicker the fabric, the longer you need to let the bleach gel set. Don't worry if it isn't perfect. Just like people, every skull is meant to be different!

✳✳✳✳✳Take It to the Next Level!✳✳✳✳✳

✳ Make several banners on matching napkins and hang them all in a row.

✳ Instead of napkins, use any kind of fabric.

✳ Make it wearable! Use the bleach pen to draw a skull on a T-shirt or jeans.

✳ Decorate a tablecloth or seat cushions.

Party with *los Muertos*

The dearly departed are excited to visit, so give respect and welcome them with a swanky soirée in their honor. Here are some magnificent *muertos* ideas to help get the party started.

Organize a personality potluck. For the sake of a communal *ofrenda,* as well as food. Ask guests to bring objects and pictures that represent their loved ones. Have each person give a blessing, and then share a story about their loved one.

Have a *calaca* cooking session. Each person brings the ingredients for a certain part of the *muertos* feast. Crank up the tunes, cook the food together, and chow down. Laminate sheets of *papel picado* for placemats. Freeze ice cubes with small skulls inside for drinks. Use *muertos* images to make small name cards. Don't forget party favors! Pass out small skull pins (found at import stores or can easily be made from polymer clay).

Use *mucho* marigolds. Make a centerpiece bouquet or place one flower on each dinner plate. String them on thread and hang as garland. Put some petals inside your party invites.

Throw a shrine-making party! Guests bring a box to decorate and dedicate to a loved one. Make sugar skulls in advance, and lay out sequins, glitter, colored foil, and tubes of icing so guests can get crafty. For an edible alternative, bake some small skull-shaped cookies or *pan de los muertos*.

Decorate. Use squeeze paints and sequins to embellish a string of skull patio lights. Dress up glassware or mugs by painting on crazy-looking skulls with glass paints.

Make some music. Burn CDs of the party's music and design a festive cover to give out so your friends will always look back on this event with warmth and happiness.

Make bread. Whip up a batch of *pan de los muertos* and bake them in the shape of skulls and decorate each one with colored icing. Paint them, package them in small bags, and give out.

I'm a movie maniac—especially films that introduce an endearing character who creates something very cool. It's not a silly guilty pleasure either. Trust me. You can actually learn a lot about design and décor by watching more than just the obvious storyline. Here are my favorite "crafty chica" pictures of all time. The movies may have had mixed reviews, but the ideas earn five stars.

And *sí*, I've tried most of these projects, and you should too!

Amélie (2001): In this French romantic comedy, a young woman (Audrey Tautou) photocopies old letters by the long-lost husband of her heartbroken landlady, cuts up the sentences, and pieces them back together as a love letter. She soaks it in tea, hangs it up on clothespins to dry, and makes it look as though it were lost in the mail for decades, thus allowing the landlady to live the rest of her life in bliss. Crafty indeed.

Chocolat (2000): A mysterious woman (Juliette Binoche) moves into a conservative French town and wreaks havoc when she opens a chocolate shop during Lent. Not only does she transform the worn-down building into an Aztec confectionary palace with cobalt blue walls and gold accents, but she also constructs an ornate village from sheets of chocolate and displays it in the storefront window.

Crazy/Beautiful (2001): A high school girl (Kirsten Dunst) turns to the dark side when her father ignores her. One of her therapies is kissing cutie-pie Jay Hernandez. The other is altering Polaroid photos. She takes two pictures and smashes them together while they are still developing. She peels them apart,

> ❝ You can actually learn a lot about design and décor by watching more than just the obvious storyline. ❞

so each picture has a bit of the other on it. She glues them in photo books and decorates them with graffiti-style marker art.

Divine Secrets of the Ya-Ya Sisterhood (2002): Ah, the Ya-Ya headdress...Every chica needs one in her crown collection. A group of little girls form their own sisterhood and construct heavy ornamental headdresses from fabric, lace, beads, pearls, brooches, and anything else they could glue on. Every time they unite for a secret meeting, even as senior citizens, they don the mighty headdresses. In addition, they build a large bulky scrapbook, dripping with ribbons and papers.

Frida (2002): Ninety-nine percent of this flick was crafty heaven. I had to see it twice in one week when it came out. The first time, all I did was soak up all the embroidery, jewelry, sugar skulls, and paintings. The second time, I actually paid attention to the story. I have yet to embroider an *almohada* (pillow) like the one Frida had on her bed, but it's on my short list of my lifetime goals.

Ghost World (2000): If you read my intro, you know why I ❤ this film. The main character (Thora Birch) is a quirky outcast who insanely doodles in her journal (yay!). Her work is very impressive as she draws caricatures of weird people she sees throughout the day. But when she has to take a remedial art class to pass high school, the art teacher dismisses her intricate illustrations as insignificant "cartoon art," and instead gives respect to a stuffy girl who glued a tampon inside a teacup and related it to the feminist movement. *Qué loco,* no?

How to Make an American Quilt (1995): A group of angstridden women of different ages and backgrounds come

together to make a wedding quilt for a confused bride-to-be. Each quilter has her own intriguing love story and weaves it into her portion of the quilt.

In America (2002): An Irish family moves to New York to start a new life. They are broke financially but rich when it comes to love and clever ideas. The witty mum (Samantha Morton) paints the apartment in wild colors, and hand-makes her daughters' adorable Halloween costumes.

Legally Blonde 2 (2003): Two snaps for the Snap Jar! Elle Woods (Reese Witherspoon) gives power to the pink movement by showing off a glittery scrapbook, as well as designing a Snap Jar. Everyone writes down something nice about another person, puts it in the decorated jar, and then draws one out and reads it out loud. I made a Snap Jar for my kids, thinking it would help bring them closer. Um, maybe this one only works best on the big screen.

Like Water for Chocolate (1992): Tita is a young woman (Lumi Cavazos) who is forbidden by her mother (Regina Torné) to marry the man she loves (Marco Leonardi), and in order to be close to her, he marries Tita's sister (Yareli Arizmendi). Tita turns to crocheting as a way to absorb her sorrows.

Lovely and Amazing (2001): One of the main characters (Catherine Keener) makes teeny tiny wooden chairs that her husband constantly steps on (by accident). She attempts to sell them, but no one wants them. She also designs wrapping paper, but that doesn't go over so well either. I love this angle because it's something all us consummate crafter wannabes can relate to. But we keep trying until something clicks—right? You bet your pom-pom fringe we do!

Pretty in Pink **(1986):** Adorable but oddball high school girl (Molly Ringwald) gets asked to the prom by a rich boy. She doesn't have a dress or money, so she reconstructs and combines two frumpy frilly dresses into a cheeky cool new one (or at least in 1986 it was).

Real Women Have Curves **(2002):** A high school student (America Ferrera) must contribute to her family's income by working at her sister's sewing factory. While there, she and a team of underpaid seamstresses are rushed to fulfill a huge order for an uncompassionate buyer. Classic scene: It's so hot in the factory that the women shed their clothing and work in their *chronies*! I'm too chicken to try this.

Selena **(1997):** Once Selena (Jennifer Lopez) gains fame on a regional level, she makes a sexy bustier to wear onstage. Her dad (Edward James Olmos) freaks out because he knows she'll be doing the washing machine dance while shaking those *chi-chis*. But Selena shows him the detailed work of gluing on all those shiny gems, and he gives her his blessing. I think that bustier needed fringe along the bottom, but that's just me.

White Oleander **(2002):** When an artist/mother (Michelle Pfeiffer) is put in prison after committing a murder, her daughter (Alison Lohman) moves from one foster home to another. The upside is the chica picked up her mother's knack for art. The girl keeps a journal and makes *impressive* paper puppets. But the gasp-worthy moment comes at the end of the

film when she displays five emotional suitcase assemblages, one for each home she lived in.

Other Crafty Movies

Confessions of a Teenage Drama Queen (2004): This comedy is trimmed with all kinds of crafty tidbits—from theater outfits to pop-up book backdrops to kitschy jewelry.

Connie and Carla (2004): Two women pose as performing drag queens, and therefore have to glam up their own clothing, à la sequins and fringe.

Ghost (1990): An artsy chica is working magic on her potter's wheel and just when her vase begins to take shape, her boyfriend comes up from behind, puts his hands on it, and destroys it. I would have kicked him.

Lost in Translation (2003): A frustrated newlywed tries to knit away her stress by stitching a scarf.

Mystery Men (1999): Clumsy superheroes take time out from training in order to sew and embellish their crime-fighting costumes.

The Notebook (2004): Rich girl makes love for the first time and then paints a canvas naked on the front porch of her lover's house.

Sound of Music (1965): A chirpy, cheery nanny makes play clothes for the children from old drapes when she is denied the funds to buy new fabric.

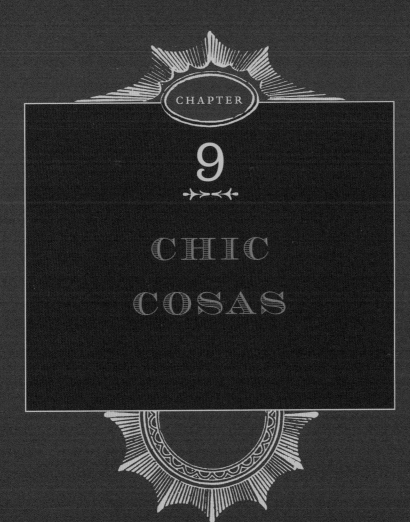

CHAPTER

9

CHIC
COSAS

One of my motives for being artsy was so I could add some Latin flair to my bedroom, living room, kitchen, and wardrobe. I'm not talking sleepy dudes in sombreros, chili peppers, or saguaro cacti. I wanted big-city, cosmopolitan chic with a dash of culture and a hint of kitsch. It was too much to ask, I guess, because I never found it. Being the ultimate optimist, I came up with my own one-of-a-kind designs. I'm sharing these with you, in the hope that it will inspire you to do the same.

L IVE, LOVE, AND PLAY. THOSE ARE WORDS TO LIVE BY—ESPECIALLY IF THEY ARE PAINTED IN SPANISH ON INEXPENSIVE CANVASES. HANG THEM ANYWHERE, IN THE OFFICE, THE BATHROOM, or the game room. Let them be a reminder to lighten up your life and soak up the sunny experiences from the day.

Supplies

3 blank canvases, 8 by 10 inches each

3 homemade word stencils

1 tube of Delta Texture Magic paint, green

Popsicle stick

Acrylic craft paint, gold and black

Craft brushes

Craft knife

1 piece of thick cardboard to line workspace

Blue painter's tape

❋ Make It ❋

1. Base-coat the canvases gold. Let dry and then add a border of black around the edges. Set aside to dry.

2. Create the stencils: Using a word processing program, choose a clean, simple font such as Futura (shown in photo) and type in your word. Increase it to approximately 150 percent. Print. Repeat for other words for other canvases.

3. Take the piece of paper and, using the cardboard as a cutting mat, carefully trace around the edges of the letters with the craft knife. Save the dots that go with "a," "o," "g," etc. Repeat for remaining words until you have three stencils. Use the blue painter's tape to affix the stencil to the canvas. Apply a small piece of tape under the dots for the "a," "o," and "g." Apply tape under any areas that are popping up. You want the stencil to be flat against the canvas.

4. Squeeze out a line of the texture paint on the Popsicle stick. With one hand, hold down the edges of the stencils around the letters, and with the other hand, smear the texture paint over the open area of the

stencil, working from right to left. Continue until entire word is covered. Quickly peel off the stencil and discard. Repeat for remaining canvases.

5. Check over the canvases and remove any stray paint with your fingernail or the edge of a paper towel. Let dry. If there is any stray paint that shows, cover it with gold paint. To highlight, add a light outline of black around the edges of the words.

Tips: Stick with a simple font: it will make the cutting much easier and will look nicer when you remove the stencil. Never cut out the letters without a piece of cardboard underneath, because you will damage your tabletop. Knead the tube of texture paint before using.

❋❋❋❋**Take It to the Next Level!**❋❋❋❋

✧ Instead of single words, stencil a favorite quote.

✧ Instead of using canvases, stencil an upbeat saying on your wall, making it a decorative border.

✧ These make great gifts for girlfriends. That way you can spread the message of having fun and living life to its fullest!

Olé! Oilcloth Tesoros Chest

O ILCLOTH IS ADDICTING. IT'S BOLD, DURABLE, AND VIBRANT, AND IT HAS MORE THAN A ZILLION USES. ALL YOU NEED IS A SEWING MACHINE AND THREAD TO COMPOSE ALL KINDS OF WEARABLES such as baby bibs, purses, and hats. For an easy route, just affix it to it a frumpy but solid box like this and watch what happens!

Supplies

1 large upright jewelry box with drawers

Assorted pieces of oilcloth, about a yard's worth

Assorted trims, about two yards' worth

Four shot glasses filled with beads

1 package of 2-part resin

Four silver cabinet knobs

Clear crystal gems

Hot glue

Screwdriver

Small handheld drill

Paper and pencil, scissors

E6000 adhesive

Make It

1. Working outside or in a well-ventilated area, mix the resin according to package directions and pour into shot glasses that are filled with beads. Tap the glasses so the resin fills in all the crevices. Set aside to cure for 24 hours.

2. Lay a piece of paper on one side of the box and trace the outline with the pencil. Repeat for all the other sides and the front of the drawers. Cut out the shapes. These are your patterns. Use them to cut out the pieces of oilcloth.

3. Cover the box with the pieces of cut oilcloth and attach with hot glue. Make sure to glue down the edges.

4. Attach trim around all the edges with the hot glue. Use screwdriver and small handheld drill to attach cabinet knobs. Add crystal gems as desired.

5. When the resin is cured inside the shot glasses, apply a generous amount of E6000 to the rims. Turn the

box upside down and press the glasses upside down in the corners of the bottom of the box. Let sit for 24 hours.

Tips: For straighter lines when cutting the oilcloth, use a rotary blade or a craft knife and cut along a ruler. To add more dimension, cut out images from the oilcloth and glue them onto contrasting panels. When mixing resin, always follow manufacturer's directions.

❈❈❈❈Take It to the Next Level!❈❈❈❈

❈ Have fun with the feet of the box. Instead of shot glasses, use large dice, round wood balls, children's alphabet blocks, etc.

❈ Search flea markets or thrift stores for more boxes to spruce up to make a matching collection in graduated sizes and shapes.

❈ Think big! Why not decorate a dresser the same way? Or better yet, cover a wood chair in oilcloth to match the box.

Casa de Cultura: You Can Do It!

From this day forward, join the crafty revolution and free yourself from the chains of a cookie-cutter lifestyle. It starts with your environment. As long as you surround yourself with personality, beauty, art, emotion, inspiration, and a bit of wackiness—that passion will follow you wherever you go. Your culture has a lot to do with it. It doesn't matter if your roots are in Cuba, Brazil, Puerto Rico, Mexico, Argentina, England, or Egypt: as long as you possess the desire, you'll triumph in finding unique ways to personalize your setting. Try these on for size.

General Tips

* Plan, but be spontaneous. Look around at your house. Take note of the places you hang out and how often. Think about what can make them more appealing in color, furniture, and décor. Play around with some sketches and then go to work on the master plan! But leave room for surprises that you find along the way.
* Don't follow trends if you don't really like them. Go with items that make you feel happy. It's your house; decorate from the heart. The ultimate purpose of your living quarters is to enrich *your* life, not that of the sales clerk at Pottery Barn.
* Think organic. Add lifelike accents such as sprawling plants, flower bouquets, a water fountain, and maybe a goldfish named Chulo. These kinds of things represent life and will generate uplifting energy in your space.
* Have a guest book handy at all times, and have your visitors sign it. Choose a theme for your book and have them leave a quote that goes with the theme. Why should guest books only be for weddings and funerals?

Design Ideas

* Buy a calendar in the theme of your homeland, favorite topic, or fantasy destination. Cut out the pictures and frame them. Line them up in rows for a modern, modular look. You can also do the same with a box of postcards.
* Collect matchbooks from your favorite countries. Color-copy the covers and glue them around a set of picture frames.
* Have an artist friend help you paint a playful mural on your backyard fence.
* Look on eBay for fabrics, postage stamps, old photos, and other foreign memorabilia that you can use in art projects.
* Buy yards of electrifying fabrics and make toss pillows for your bed or sofa.
* Always keep music in the background. Turn off the TV and play your favorite artists while you cook, clean, and entertain company.
* Visit antique stores to find vintage Latin imports such as salt and pepper shakers, cookie jars, old books, handbags, and more.
* Make a travel scrapbook of your trips and leave it on the coffee table.
* Pick up some inexpensive wood furniture and go crazy painting it! Don't forget to add several coats of varnish so it won't chip.
* Collect Spanish or other foreign-language magazines and decoupage them on tabletops, seats, frames, and more.

The Chocolate Club

Crafts and chocolate are my two guilty pleasures in life. As a plus-size *mamacita,* I have a fridge full of humiliating food stories. I've been denied cake at the office party in front of the entire staff, I've lost and gained weight more times than Anna Nicole Smith, I've ordered a dessert for my invisible "friend" at coffeehouses; the list goes on. None of those tops the agony I experienced as a member of the office Chocolate Club.

I had been in the department only a few months. One day, I was chatting with the very sweet lady who sat next to me. We were comparing our devotion to all things that contained cocoa. I sang her a song I wrote about tuxedo cheesecake and she recited a haiku about hazelnut truffles. We giggled and shared an espresso brownie. It was the best co-worker bonding moment I've ever had.

She licked the crumbs from her finger and raised an eyebrow. "I'll let you in on a secret, Kathy. A few of us here put together a 'chocolate club.' If you want, I'll put in a good word for you. It's very exclusive."

"I want! I want!" I chanted as I licked the icing from the brownie wrapper. She wouldn't give me the names of the members, but explained that one of them is the designated keeper of the chocolate. Any member in good standing could, at any time, request a piece and get it. Since I was the newbie on staff, this act of graciousness made me feel like one of the team.

Two weeks passed and I lost hope for my acceptance. My neighbor and I hadn't shared any more brownies and she never mentioned my pending status.

> ❦ 'I'll let you in on a secret, Kathy. A few of us here put together a "chocolate club." If you want, I'll put in a good word for you. It's very exclusive.' ❧

"Forever the outsider, always the loner," I thought.

As a way to express my pain, I made a drastic, melodramatic decision. I started the Atkins diet and made an elaborate diet shrine that was trimmed in Pez candies and red hots.

A couple weeks went by and I was asked to cover for Bonnie, the TV book lady. It was a big deal. She had a detailed job that involved a PC, a Mac, and compiling multiple pages of TV channel statistics. It was more dreadful than giving up warm French bread for my new diet. Bonnie was a woman who stuffed fifty hours of error-free duties into a forty hour week. She went off to frolic in Hawaii, and I was expected to fill her shoes for a week.

By 10 a.m. the first day, Monday, I was lost. Nothing was working, I forgot everything I had learned, and no one on the staff knew how to fix it. To pass time while waiting for help, I peeked in Bonnie's desk drawers. I wasn't in search of anything in particular, but I found something. Something grand.

"Ah hah! It seems our perfect Bonnie has a dirty little secret!" I whispered as I poked the naughty goods with her silver letter opener. There in the bottom drawer, stuffed *waaay* in the back, were several bags and boxes of gourmet chocolates. The good stuff. Imported. But I couldn't indulge. I had lost a few inches on Atkins already: why would I tamper with that?

But the stress of the job caused my mouth to water for the chocolates. I opened the drawer, clawed the bags to the forefront, and scooped out a handful of wrapped chocolates. That's how the next two days went. Whenever I was stumped

with the job, I munched on chocolates. It was much-needed therapy and it calmed my nerves. I didn't care until Wednesday morning came and the chocolates were just about gone. Bonnie was due back on Friday.

"Ahhh, no biggie. I'll replace them tomorrow before she gets back," I concluded. Later that afternoon, one of my co-workers came up to me at Bonnie's desk.

"Hi, Kathy! It's time for the Chocolate Club!" he said with a bright, enthusiastic smile.

I clapped my chubby hands together and squealed, "Oh goodie!" because I had finally been approved for this exclusive treat. It was good timing because I had just polished off the last of the treats in the TV lady's stash.

"Where do we go to get it? This is so exciting!" I said as I scooted my chair back, ready to follow him.

"Oh, well, Bonnie is the keeper of the Chocolate Club's chocolate," he said. "She stores it under tight surveillance at the back of that drawer down there. You can just hand me a bag and I'll go pass it out to the others."

Um, whoops...

I couldn't get any words out of my mouth. So I sat there with a blank stare and a slow blink. All that came to mind was that I was the New Girl Who Ate All the Chocolate Club's Chocolate. And how in the name of the Blessed Mother of Mosaics was I going to get out of this, and retain any shred of competent co-worker dignity?

He was stared back with an expression that said, "Hello? Do you speaka English? Gimme the chocolate, missy!"

I didn't think these words, but they came out of my mouth

anyway: "I am SO sorry...I think...I ate it all. I didn't know all the chocolate belonged to the Chocolate Club, and I got stressed with Bonnie's job and I started nibbling and..."

He shifted off his leg and straightened his posture. "You ate ALL that chocolate. In TWO days? It's all GONE?"

"Yes. It's gone. Please don't tell the other members," I said through my hands that covered my face. "I was planning on replacing it by the time Bonnie came back."

"No prob," he said. He walked away and that was the end of it. Or so I thought.

Thursday, he returned. He rested his elbow on top of the computer monitor. He looked down and delivered the bad news: "We've been talking and well, we don't think we want to add any more people to the Chocolate Club right now. Please don't take it personally."

I gulped to hold back the tears. "OK. I understand. Thanks anyway."

It was the *most* traumatic chunky girl moment in my life. I was exiled from the Chocolate Club. No one ever brought up the experience again. And the next time I filled in for Bonnie, the stash was gone. Years later, I asked the nice lady who had originally invited me into the club about it. Turns out they killed the club shortly after the incident, for reasons I don't know of. Reasons I don't want to know of!

「「 'We've been talking and well, we don't think we want to add any more people to the Chocolate Club right now. Please don't take it personally.' **」」**

Crafty Chica's Lesson Learned: A club can be a nurturing chapter in your life, but only if you know the details. Whether it's chocolate or crafting, ask questions before you commit. Get to know the members; think about what you have to gain from being a member. If you can't find a club that suits your character, form your own. And of course, if you ever fill in for a co-worker, stay out of their drawers.

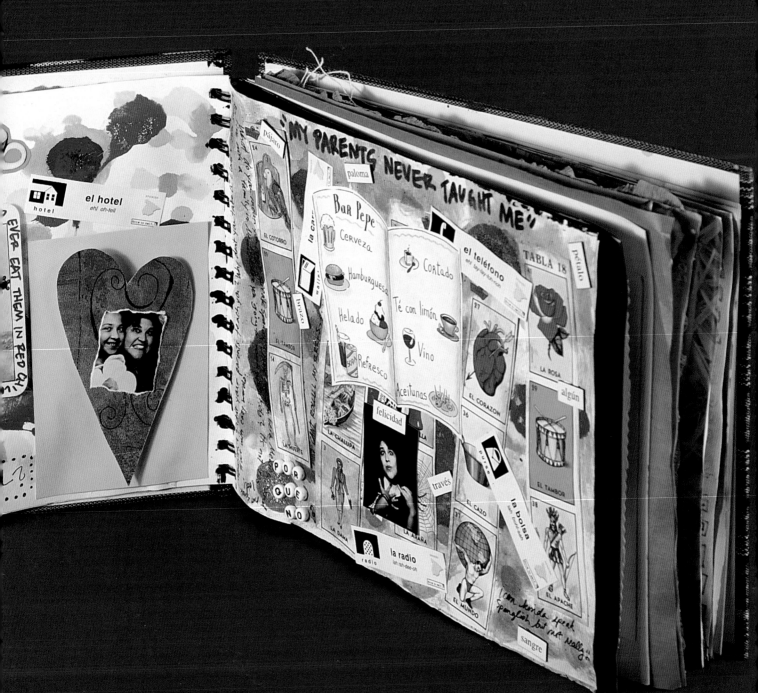

CHAPTER

10

COZY COMADRES

Playing with paints and sketchbooks is healthy and insightful as a solo hobby. But don't forget that there is power in numbers. A rowdy girls' night out is also healthy and insightful. Only your *comadres* will tell it like it is. They'll stop you from cheating on your diet, help you find a man, and let you use their most sacred collection of Swarovski crystals on your craft project. Your last assignment of this book is to throw a kickin' fiesta with all your artsy gal pals. Start with these friendship-friendly activities and continue on. Check out page 177 to learn how to start your own craft group.

I N HIGH SCHOOL, YOUR WHOLE WORLD REVOLVES AROUND FRIENDS AND FUN. THAT ALL CHANGES WHEN YOU START COLLEGE, GET MARRIED, HAVE KIDS, AND GO TO WORK. THAT DOESN'T MEAN YOU have to give up your girl time. You just have to learn how to savor it. Here is a one way to do that, either at a craft party or solo, so everyone can work at home at her own pace. Each friend creates a scrapbook spread, all about them. If there are five crafty chicas in your group, each person makes five spreads. Give out those four and you'll get four in return. Attach the pages inside a superb scrapbook that you embellished for this special cause. Don't forget to make a set for you to start off the book!

Supplies

1 scrapbook

2 pieces of scrapbook paper, 12 by 12 inches each

Assorted pieces of decorative paper

Assorted card stock

Assorted personal photos of yourself, doing things you love, or posing with people you love

Embellishments: tags, rubber stamps, embossing powders, stickers, small grommets, ink pens, fibers

Assorted decorative edge scissors, hole punches, die cuts

Glue sticks

Make It

1. Choose your favorite color for the two pieces of scrapbook paper that you will use for the background of your spread. Select one anchor (largest picture on the spread) picture of you, and then smaller accent photos. Make color copies of original photos, and enlarge and reduce as desired.

2. Choose colored card stock to line the back of your photos. These will not only support your photos, but will add a nice frame to them as well. Cut to size and then use the glue stick to adhere the copies of photos to the card stock.

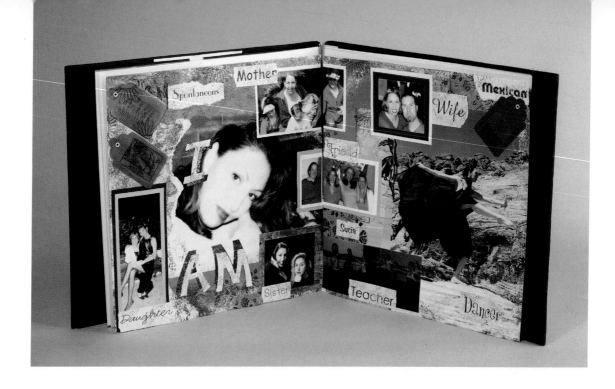

3. Now that you have all your photos, arrange them on the page in an appealing fashion. Leave room to add a headline for your spread. Glue the pictures in place.

4. Create a main headline and smaller headings by using rub-on letters, stencils, rubber stamps, stickers, or freehand drawing with ink pens. Line the back with card stock and glue in place.

5. Fill in with other embellishments as desired. Trade your pages with your friends and insert them in your scrapbook.

Tips: Always arrange—and rearrange—your scrapbook layouts. Even if you have a gut urge to glue on impulse, it doesn't hurt to try your options and play around with the layout. You want it to be spontaneous but balanced at the same time. Always apply your paper objects with a glue stick to keep your pages crisp and flat. Stick with acid-free glues, papers, and embellishments.

Sassy Secrets of Scrapbooking

Scrapbook supplies are everywhere—and everyone seems to be doing it. But where to start? Here are a few methods to the madness:

* As you choose your photos, write the event, date, and place on a sticky note and attach it to the back. Store them in clean boxes.
* If you have many photos from the same event, lay them out on a table and narrow down your choices. Look for clear, crisp images that show emotion and action.
* Brainstorm headlines. Look at the pictures and try to come up with a short phrase that captures the essence. Scribble down as many word combinations that you think of. Eventually one will be perfect!
* Crop your photos. Place your thumb and index fingers together from each hand. Set it over your images to find the best portion. Use a straightedge to trim excess paper.
* Before you start, make a mini-outline of the book and the pages you want to make: subject of scrapbook, color scheme, embellishments you want to use. This will help you stay focused.
* If you are just starting out, try using one big picture instead of a bunch of small ones.
* Super-size it! Instead of using a standard-size page, create a scrapbook layout on a canvas that you can hang on the wall.
* Scrapbooking isn't only about the big events in life, it's also about the little day-to-day ventures: drinking coffee with a friend, babysitting your nieces, revamping your bedroom…all of these will make engaging layouts!

✳✳✳ Take It to the Next Level! ✳✳✳

✳ Make an opening and/or index page for your album.
✳ Save things like ticket stubs of movies you went to with your friends, titles of books you read, and mementos of other friendship adventures, and incorporate them in your layout.
✳ Include a place on your spread to add journaling. Leave an open space of card stock to share a poem or a funny story based on your friendship.
✳ When you trade your pages with your friend, give her a little box filled with some of your favorite scrapbook decorations so she can use them in her future pages.

Girly-girl Photo Book

S URE, WE *MUJERS* WANT JUSTICE AND EQUALITY, BUT THAT DOESN'T MEAN WE HAVE TO SKIMP ON FEMININITY. CELEBRATE YOUR INNER GIRLY-GIRL BY ASSEMBLING THIS FETCHING PINT-SIZE photo book. Use the "she-ro" theme by using female-themed stamps, stickers, and papers. You can fill it with pictures of women that inspire you like Celia Cruz, Frida Kahlo, Mother Teresa, Maya Angelou, Selena, your mother, daughter, nana . . .

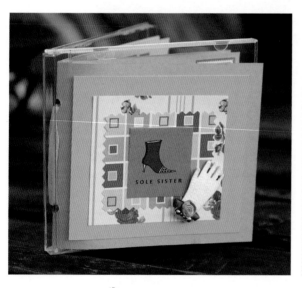

Supplies

1 empty CD jewel case

3 pieces of colored card stock, 9½ by 4½ inches each

6 pieces of contrasting but color-coordinated patterned paper, 4 by 4 inches

Assorted strips of patterned paper for embellishing

Hole puncher

1 piece of ribbon, 8 inches long

1 piece of ribbon, 12 inches long

Assorted rubber stamps, stickers, embellishments

Color copies or instant camera photos from girly outings (spa days, lunches, nightclubbing, bunko night, etc.)

Glue stick

Scissors

* Make It *

1. Take the three pieces of colored card stock and fold them down the center. Sharpen the creases with a bone folder or the back of a spoon, so they are nice and sharp. Insert them inside each other, to create a book.

2. Tear the edges of the smaller strips of paper and glue them along the inner edges of the pages to add more texture. Add rubber-stamped designs, stickers, etc., to all the pages. Add the photos and, if you want, write funny captions to go with them. Decorate the cover.

3. Punch a hole in each end of the spine. Thread the smaller piece of ribbon through and tie in a knot on the outside of the spine.

4. Place the book inside the jewel case. If you want, slide the cover through the open slot in the hinge of the case, so it rests outside the case, but the rest of the book is inside. Tie the long piece of ribbon around the entire book and store in a safe, happy place.

Tips: For perfect sizing, use a mini-camera, such as an i-Zone: the pictures come with sticky backs so you can attach them easily. Trim your pages as needed to make them line up evenly. Do not make your embellishments too thick: you want them to fit neatly in the jewel case.

❋❋❋❋❋Take It to the Next Level!❋❋❋❋❋

✧ Talk about way cool party favors! These are inexpensive to make. You can pass them out at your next soirée, and leave i-Zones on the tables so people can build them throughout the night.

✧ Make a CD of all your friends' favorite songs and decorate a cover to match. Keep the photo book and CD together, and *bam!* You have a multimedia set of friendship memories.

✧ Use the book to log your favorite movies, quotes, or book titles. Jot down topics of conversations and jokes, etc.

Hardback Book Purse

J UICY NOVELS ARE A WAY TO ESCAPE FROM A HUMDRUM WORLD AND LIVE A WILD, CAREFREE LIFE. AND THEN THERE ARE THOSE "IFFY" BOOKS THAT PILE UP AT THE THRIFT STORE, ALL SAD AND dusty waiting for someone to pay 50¢ and take them home. It's never gonna happen! That is unless you save a book by recycling it into a darling handbag. Don't take just any hardback, though. Cruise the shelves for cheap homeless hardbacks with good structure and give them a second chance at being hip.

Supplies

1 thick hardback book, preferably with a Latino theme or author	Craft knife
	Scissors
	Measuring tape
Fabric	Straight pins
Purse handles	Foam craft brush
Handheld drill	Strong ribbed ribbon
Glues: Hot glue, E6000, and white craft glue	Fringe, cut-out images from fabric (optional)

Make It

1. Remove the guts of the book: Opening the cover of the book. Gently run the craft knife down the seams, cutting the binding on both sides. Be careful not to cut through the cover spine. Save the guts of the book to read later or to use in a future craft project.
2. Make the lining of the purse: Open the book and measure the width from end to end. Cut a piece of fabric to match, but add a half inch on each side. Fold the edges over, pin in place, and sew. Trim excess fabric. Set lining aside for step 5.
3. Make the sides of the purse:
    * Rest the book flat on its spine with the covers upright. Hold the covers in place so you can measure vertically from the bottom to the top. Now measure the sides plus the empty space between the covers.

* Cut four pieces of fabric to match these measurements, but add 2 inches to each side.
* Separate the fabric into two sets of two. On one set, pin a half-inch hem all the way around and sew two pieces together, right side out. This will give a nice polished look to the edges for your finished purse. Repeat for the other set. You now have the side panels for the purse.
* Hot-glue the panels in place: Place the book on its spine, covers standing upright. Center the panel into place, making sure to line up the fabric panel so it covers the side and the inside of the spine. The extra fabric on the panel will allow you to open the purse as wide as you need to. Glue the bottom portion of the fabric panel to the inner spine, and then up the inner ridges of the covers. Hold in place until glue cools.

4. Cut four pieces of the ribbon (two for each side of the purse). Attach the purse handles by folding a piece of ribbon in half and inserting the handle through it. Use E6000 to glue the ends of the ribbon to the inside of the purse. Add a drop of hot glue to hold it in place. Repeat until both handles are secured. Let dry for a few hours.

5. Use the craft brush and white craft glue to "paint" the entire inside area of the purse. Take the fabric from step 2 and insert it inside the purse. Use your fingers or a chopstick to push the fabric into the corners of the purse. This will cover the entire inside surface. Smooth it out with your hands, so it is wrinkle-free. Let dry.

6. Give your purse a detailed inspection. Check for any edges where the fabric has lifted and secure it with hot glue. Embellish the front as desired.

Tips: Buy your book at the thrift store or used bookstore; they are cheap and you can pick up a few. When choosing a book for this project, always consider the thickness of the book. The wider it is, the more things it will hold. This project works best if you have a friend helping out: if not, you can still master it solo. If you buy an old book and the cover is dirty, use a damp cloth to wipe it down. If you are picky about recycling a vintage book, have it appraised to make yourself feel better!

✳✳✳✳**Take It to the Next Level!**✳✳✳✳

✤ Add a clasp so you can close your purse.

✤ Line the outside of the book, as well as the inside.

✤ Visit your local fabric or craft store to get ideas on hip handles and ways to attach them.

✤ Decoupage the outside of your purse with vintage-looking images.

Craft It Up with Your Own Group!

Whether you're a part-time artist, a dabbler of decoupage, or a full-on glue-gun-totin' craftaholic like me, you must join or form a craft group, like, today. Words can't describe how much kooky fun it is to gather a group of wildly creative women and set them loose at a table of art supplies and conversation. The "Oh. My. God. No way!" stories take on a life of their own, the laughter machine unloads, and glitter flies everywhere. At times there are even tears shed for one another's achievements and heartaches. And it all wraps up with a show-and-tell finale, where each person takes a turn to hold up her piece and brag about it. Excited? You should be. Here are the basics for starting your own group.

Round 'em Up

How does one find like-minded souls? Keep it simple. Shake the tree—send a note out to family and friends (you'll know which ones will be interested!), explaining what you want to do. Ask them if they would like to take part in a monthly spectacular crafty lady bash. If you feel daring, look for people outside of your normal social circles. Post note cards at craft stores, colleges, or libraries. It's a groovy way to make new *comadres,* and the varying styles will add a nice flavor to the clique. When you have four to six (no more than eight) willing souls, set up an e-mail list or online message group so everyone can post important dates, notes, pictures, and messages.

What to Do?

Alrighty, you have the members—now what? Find your common interests. Is everyone into needle arts like knitting and sewing? Or perhaps collage art and paper crafts? Most crafters enjoy trying out new techniques, which is why these groups have so much to offer. Lucy can show Cici how to knit. Cici can show Diana how to make a French knot with embroidery thread. Here are several more successful ideas based on my experience.

What to make: Two to three hours is a good time frame to yak, eat, and complete a project. Generally, most crafts work well as group projects. Some of my favorites are cigar box shrines, artist trading cards, matchbox shrines, decoupaged boxes or frames, easy handmade books, beading, knitting, and embroidery. You can even rent a "how-to" video and everyone can watch and learn together. It's common that some chicas don't finish their projects in time; if that happens to you, don't worry! Just take it home.

Where to meet: There are two ways that work really well. The first is to have a different person host the meeting each month. The host supplies the basics: glue, paper towels, scissors, ruler, paints, craft knife, etc. The other option is to make it a field trip every month. You can meet at the park, the food court at the mall, an open lab at a craft store, even a coffeehouse.

What to bring: Make it a crafty potluck. Each person brings a food or drink offering, a small bag of craft supplies to share, basic tools (favorite scissors, pens, stamps, etc.), and whatever items she wants to use for her piece. It's more interesting when everyone brings their current favorite CD. It keeps the music going and you get exposed to new tunes.

Other Ideas

Take a class together. You can keep the group lively by enrolling together in a class at a local arts and craft store. This option is perfect for tapping into new trends and practicing difficult techniques, because a know-it-all instructor is right there to help!

Name your group. Have everyone submit ideas and choose one out of a hat or vote. Nominate someone to design a tantalizing logo. Come up with a catchy tagline for your group.

Set up a Web site. Start a group blog or an actual site. Give everyone their own page with a personality questionnaire. If your members have Web sites, promote them. Include a page that links to other craft groups in your community or around the country. Post pictures of completed projects, along with instructions. Any lessons you've learned, post them to inspire other crafters.

Throw a collaborative art show. Check if your community has First Fridays (a night where all the galleries host openings). If so, visit local art spaces and pitch an idea for a show that unites all of your work.

Become crafty heroes for one another. If someone in your group is in dire need with a home-renovating project, centerpieces to assemble, or a room to redo before out-of-town company arrives, devote a meeting to helping out. You'll find this will also extend to help with relationships, cooking, and other areas of life.

Buy an art booth at a festival. The trouble with art shows is that the fees can be high, and it's stressful to work the crowd all day. By joining forces like the artful wonder women you are, you can cut down on all of that.

Design and create for charity. Sew or knit blankets for a local shelter, or volunteer as a group for fund-raising events.

Invite mystery guests. Meet a talented artist in your travels? Invite them to come to a meeting and join in.

Take oodles of pictures. These will come in handy for the projects in this book. Post the pictures on your Web site so the world can see how brilliant you all are!

Pick themes for your meeting. Celebrate one another's backgrounds and upbringings. Have Cuban day one month and Texas day the next. You get the idea!

All About You!

If you've reached this page, that means you now know my
devastating secrets. The only way to make this fair is for you
to cough up one of your *loca artista* adventures right here.
You know you have a good one! If not, then use these pages
to create a scrapbook, take notes, doodle, make crafty to-do
lists, or whatever else tickles you.

_____

_____

_____

_____

_____

_____

_____

_____

_____

_____

_____

_____

_____

Templates

HERE ARE THE TEMPLATES FOR SEVERAL PROJECTS IN THIS BOOK.

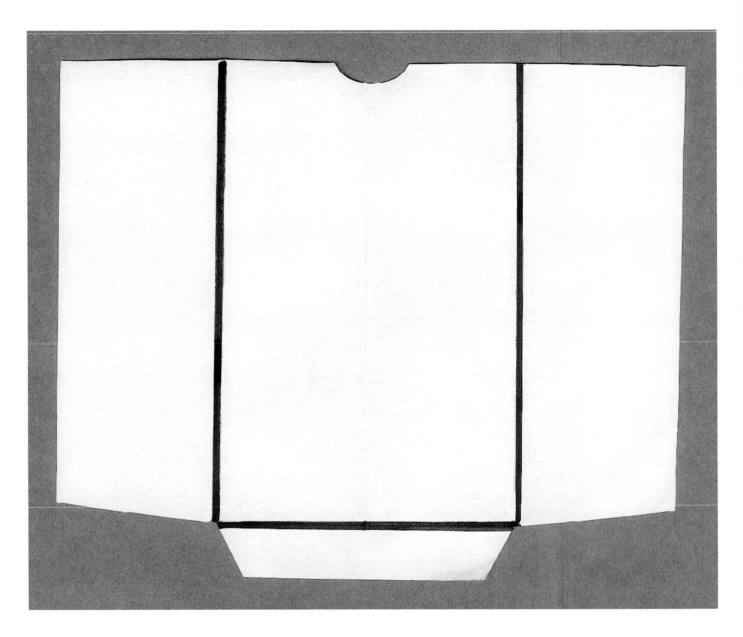

To use the envelope template, scale it up to 200% on a photocopier.

Resources and Suppliers

LOOKIE CHICAS, HERE IS MY LIST OF ALL THE TREASURES I'VE DISCOVERED THROUGHOUT THE YEARS. TAKE TIME TO CHECK THEM OUT, YOU WON'T REGRET IT!

Books About Living a Creative, Crafty Life

Get Crafty: Hip Home Ec, by Jean Railla (Broadway Books, 2004)

The Latina's Bible, by Sandra Guzmán (Three Rivers Press, 2002)

Living Out Loud: Activities to Fuel a Creative Life, by Keri Smith (Chronicle Books, 2004)

The Starving Artist's Way: Easy Projects for Low-Budget Living, by Nava Lubelski (Three Rivers Press, 2004)

Stitch N Bitch: The Knitter's Handbook, by Debbie Stoller (Workman Publishing, 2003)

Wild with a Glue Gun: Getting Together with Crafty Friends, by Christine Stickler and Kitty Harmon (Northlight Books, 2004)

Web Sites to Spark Your *Chispa*

Another Girl at Play
www.another.girlatplay.com
This upbeat site showcases artistic women and the muses that inspire them. Includes interviews with each personality.

Artella...The Waltz of Words and Art
www.artellawordsandart.com
An online magazine for artists and writers. Offers creativity exercises and workshops.

Be Jane DIY Home Improvement
www.be-jane.com
Empowering home improvement site for women.

BUST Magazine
www.bust.com
For feminist edgy chicas who like to craft *and* kick butt.

Camp SARK
www.campsark.com
Dedicated to helping men and women find their inner child.

Comadre Coaching
www.comadrecoaching.com
Life coaching with *corazón* for artsy types.
Includes tips and exercises to help reach your
personal goals.

Craftster.org
www.craftster.org
A huge community of clever crafters who post
their ideas and pictures of completed projects.

Crafty Chica
www.craftychica.com
My Web site, offering free craft projects, articles
on crafting trends, creativity tips, and *mucho
mas!*

Diva Tribe
www.divatribe.com
A community and resource site for smart, coura-
geous, and artistic women.

Empowerment 4 Women
www.empowerment4women.org/
A spiritual, motivational site for women.

Get Crafty
www.getcrafty.com
Making art out of everyday life from cooking
and cleaning to crafting and clubbing.

Hungry Girl
www.hungry-girl.com
Funny, flashy, and fashionable nutrition site.
Chocked with great healthy habits!

Knitty
www.knitty.com
Little purls of wisdom and hip project patterns
for the modern knitter.

Latina/o Art Community
latinoartcommunity.org/community/LAC.html
Directory of Latino/a artists.

Our Lady of Weight Loss
www.ourladyofweightloss.com
Offers perky and professional techniques on how
to use art as a method of weight loss.

Purse Stories
www.pursestories.com
Entertaining site where women write and post
stories about their favorite accessory of all
time—purses!

Put Down the Donut
www.putdownthedonut.com
Quirky and insightful weight loss site.

Skirt! Magazine
www.skirtmag.com
A saucy site for sassy ladies that love to play,
dream, shop and work.

Supernaturale
www.supernaturale.com
A cyber gathering place for creative, crafty, and
clever women.

The Switchboards
www.theswitchboards.com
Directory and community site for arts and crafts
business owners.

Two Peas in a Bucket
www.twopeasinabucket.com
Crafty ideas and challenges galore.

Craft Groups and Organizations

American Craft Council
www.craftcouncil.org

Church of Craft
www.churchofcraft.org

Craft and Hobby Association
www.hobby.org

Craft Yarn Council of America
www.craftyarncouncil.com

Crochet Guild of America
www.crochet.org

Home Sewing Association
www.sewing.org

Suppliers and Contributors

Anima Designs
Vintage photos
www.animadesigns.com

The Bead Museum Shop
Coral, turquoise beads, findings
5754 W. Glenn Dr.
Glendale, AZ 85301
(623) 931-2737
www.thebeadmuseum.com

Bella Brava
Love potion recipes
www.bellabrava.com

Chica Clothing
Latina T-shirts
www.chica1.com

The Creative Iron
Iron-on fabric borders
www.stensource.com/creativeiron

The Creative Quest
Papers, rubber stamps
7146 N. 57th Dr.
Glendale, AZ 85301
(623) 847-2215
www.thecreativequest.com

Delta Technical Coatings
Paints, general craft supplies
www.deltacrafts.com

Día de los Muertos
Trivia, history, video, photos, and more
www.azcentral.com/ent/dead

Diane Ribbon and Notions
General craft supplies
2319 W. Holly St.
Phoenix AZ 85009
(602) 271-9273
www.dianeribbon.com

Duncan Crafts
General Craft Supplies
www.duncancrafts.com

eBay
Assorted supplies
www.ebay.com

Fry's Marketplace
General housewares, glass jars, imported juice
cans
www.frysfood.com

Goodwill Industries International
Fabric remnants, jean jackets
www.goodwill.org

The Home Depot
General supplies and tools, supplies for soldering, basic hardware
www.homedepot.com

IKEA
Mirror, shrine box
www.ikea.com

Jo-Ann Fabric and Crafts
www.joann.com

Lotería Workshop
www.lotmex.com

Making Memories
Scrapbook supplies, stickers, phrases
www.makingmemories.com

Mexican Sugar Skull
Molds for skulls
www.mexicansugarskull.com

Michaels
General craft supplies
www.michaels.com

Pier 1 Imports
Silverware tray, tea tray, glass jars
www.pier1.com

Printed Treasures
Inkjet printable fabric
www.printedtreasures.com

Silver Crow Creations
Embellishments for shadow boxes
www.silvercrowcreations.com

Stampington & Company
Embellishments
www.stampington.com

St. Theresa Textile Trove
Mexican-themed fabrics, oilcloth, trims
1329 Main St.
Cincinnati, OH 45210
(800) 236-2450
www.sttheresatextile.com

Suenos Latin American Imports
Small import items
6035 N. 7th Street
Phoenix, AZ 85014
www.milagromercado.com
www.dayofthedeadmercado.com

Target
General supplies
www.target.com

10 Seconds Studio
Embossing tin, tools
www.tensecondsstudio.com

Props & Acknowledgments

SPECIAL THANKS TO all my Aztec Warrior Angels who helped make this book happen! *Abrazos con glitter* to my husband Patrick for being my best friend, husband, and, now, personal illustrator! I wouldn't be doing any of this without him. Any time I ever doubted myself, he found a way to make me feel like I'm worth a million bucks. My kids, DeAngelo and Maya, I love you so much and I'm sorry this book took so much time away from our family-bonding adventures. Both of you were so kind and patient with me, I'm so proud of both of you. And, yup: I owe you big-time!

I'm grateful for my other family members as well. *Número uno:* My sister Theresa Cano. *Muchas gracias* for not yelling at me when I called you every other night at 2 a.m. to bounce a craft idea off of you . . . I hope some day you get into crafting too; girl, you are missing out! Lots of hugs to my mom and dad, Norma and David Cano; my brother and sister-in-law, David and Michelle Cano; my mom-in-law, Susie Murillo: and the Hadleys and the Garcias.

My crafty *amigas* were a big help too. *Viva!* to my craft group, the Phoenix Fridas: Tracy Dove, Anita Mabante-Leach, Keri Plezia, Leticia Amezaga, Carmen Guerrero, and Carrie Wheeler. And my other *comadres:* Laurie Notaro, Jean Railla, Randy Cordova, Bill and Deborah Muller, Alisa Valdes-Rodriguez, Mary Castillo, Marcela Landres, Nancy Marmolejo, Jenny Hart, Michelle Savoy, Maria Fowler, Ashley Farmer, Shannon Johnson, Jaimee Rose, Sadie Jo Smokey, and Terri Ouellette. Thank you to Zada Blayton for launching my professional craft career by giving me a weekly craft column. Special hugs to my writing group: Robrt Pela, Camille Kimball, Abigail Beshkin, and Pamela Chanko.

I had help on some of projects and much appreciation goes to John Samora (Flamin' Firepot), Anita Mabante-Leach (Flamenco Fringe Tanks), Lorinda Morales (Potions for *Pasion*), and Melissa Gould (Scrap N Swap Memory Album). Thank you to Denise Icard for providing the patterns for the tag book, paper lights, and photo book; and Robrt Pela for the wickedly cool collage table idea.

Glitter sprinkles to *Las Sucias;* my artsy *amigas* at GetCrafty.com, Supernaturale.com and Craftster.org; the crew at Diane Ribbon and Notions (Arizona's oldest crafts warehouse, thirty years strong!); the *Arizona Midday* crew at KPNX (thank you, Amy!); the *Arizona Republic*'s Kerry Lengel, Nicole Carroll, Stacy Sullivan, Tami Thornton, Keira Nothaft, and Randy Lovely for always supporting my crafty endeavors outside of the newsroom. *Muchas gracias* to Margaret Beardsley and the *Good Morning Arizona* 3'TV team. A good-karma glitter shrine goes out to my agents at the William Morris Agency, Scott Wachs and Jonathan Pecarsky. You make my dreams come true!

And to the person who robbed me at the craft store while I was working on this book, I forgive you. Most of all, a big thank you, John Samora, for the *muy perfecto* photography, and Rene Alegria, Andrea Montejo, and the rest of the staff at Rayo Books and HarperCollins for putting it all together.

Kathy Cano Murillo lives in Phoenix, Arizona, and is an admitted craftaholic. She not only has tasted three kinds of glitter, sipped her paint water, used a glue stick for Chapstick, and flaunted two nasty glue-gun burn scars, but she also took her formerly gorgeous living room and turned it into the family art studio. She is a professional craft designer, a national craft columnist, and entertainment reporter for the *Arizona Republic*. She has authored four other books, including *Making Shadow Boxes & Shrines, La Casa Loca: Latino Style Comes Home,* and the popular tween *Crafty Diva* series, and also runs the popular Web site CraftyChica.com. She recently finished her first novel.

Patrick Murillo is the illustrator of this book and Kathy's husband. He has designed merchandise for Lowe's Home Improvement Stores and is known for his comical *Día de los Muertos* sculptures and paintings. When he isn't in the family's living-room-turned-art-studio, he writes and records *reggae en español*. Patrick and Kathy have two kids, DeAngelo and Maya, and three Chihuahuas, Ozzy, Bianca, and Cha-Cha. Visit his Web site at www.patrickmurillo.com.

John Samora is a commercial photographer based in Phoenix, Arizona. His clients include Fender Musical Instruments, Capitol Records, *Sunset Magazine, Time, The National Geographic, Glamour,* and more. He also fronts the blues band Big Nick and the Gila Monsters. His Web site is at www.johnsamora.com.

FIN